Shakespeare's
Dramatic Structures

Shakespeare's
Dramatic Structures

Anthony Brennan

Routledge & Kegan Paul
London, Boston and Henley

First published in 1986
by Routledge & Kegan Paul plc

14 Leicester Square, London WC2H 7PH, England

9 Park Street, Boston, Mass. 02108, USA and

Broadway House, Newtown Road,
Henley on Thames, Oxon RG9 1EN, England

Set in Plantin, 10 on 12pt
by Inforum Ltd of Portsmouth
and printed in Great Britain
by Billing and Sons Ltd,
Worcester

Library of Congress Cataloging in Publication Data

Brennan, Anthony

Shakespeare's dramatic structures.
Bibliography: p.
Includes index.
1. Shakespeare, William, 1564–1616——Technique.
2. Shakespeare, William, 1564–1616——Criticism and
interpretation. I. Title.
PR2995.B68   1986   822.3'3   85–10857

ISBN 0–7102–0450–7

British Library CIP data also available

Contents

Preface

I am concerned here with two of the strategies which Shakespeare developed in structuring his plays to ensure their compelling effect on a theatre audience. The techniques have been noted and commented on by many scholars. I wish here to examine the variety of ways in which Shakespeare exploited basic techniques of structural design until, transformed by his ingenuity, they become as recognizable a part of his signature as the dense poetic texture produced by his clusters of imagery. Shakespeare's skills in structuring plays have, until recent years, been given only spasmodic and inconsistent attention in interpretations of his work. There have been decades even in this century when Shakespeare's connection with the theatre appeared to be a skeleton in the closet that polite family members discreetly ignored. I am grateful to the many renegades who resisted the idea, broached by the Chorus of *Henry V* and latched on to by so many scholars, that our muse of fire could be best appreciated only if we dispensed with the unworthy scaffold on which he brought forth the great objects of his invention. Among those who considered theatre as capable of more than inexplicable dumb shows and noise in revealing what Shakespeare is up to I value A. C. Bradley, R. G. Moulton, A. C. Sprague, N. Coghill, S. L. Bethell, W. J. Lawrence and H. T. Price. A host of critics have, in the last two decades, spent a great deal of time in trying to understand what pressures and traditions helped to influence the composition of Shakespeare's plays and how they are designed to achieve their impact in live performance. I have enjoyed the work of Bernard Beckerman, Muriel Bradbrook, Alan Dessen, Madeleine Doran, Alfred Harbage, Emrys Jones, Maynard Mack, Mark Rose, J. L. Styan, James Hirsch and the many others who help to define the precision of construction in the plays which must have provoked more variety of interpretations in performance than the rest of the world's drama put together.

The texts I have used in my analysis are the single editions of the Pelican Shakespeare. The Pelican texts, besides being generally available and convenient to handle for my purposes, also benefit from the consistent general editorship of Alfred Harbage whose recognition of the importance of construction in Shakespeare's plays is reflected in the clarity of the presentation of the texts.

It is still quite a common experience in meetings on Shakespeare which bring theatre people and literary scholars together to observe how quickly, out of mutual suspicion, icicles begin to form on the ceiling. These studies owe a debt of gratitude not only to the scholars listed above. My most extensive debt is to the countless actors and directors who have caught in a gesture, a grouping of characters, the articulation of the action within a scene, or the organization of a whole production the rhythm, the mood, the pace and all the elements of design that make the play work. I cannot sympathize with the critic who prefers to confine himself to the ideal productions he can work up in his own mind. That is merely to make do, like Hamlet, with the chameleon's dish and to 'eat the air, promise-cramm'd', or like Kate to be fed only 'with the very name of meat'. I owe a great deal of the pleasure I take in the varied dishes within and among Shakespeare's plays to the dedicated skills of theatre people who have served them up to me so frequently with new revelations of their savours. I am trying here to repay a little of that debt.

Introduction

Works designed to be presented in live performance usually have a structural organization which allows them to capitalize on the fact that they have the audience's attention for a more or less continuous and limited period of time. Poets and novelists usually develop variety of material, tempo and mood but they are not under quite the same compelling force to provide them as playwrights are. A reader can choose to provide variety for himself by setting a book aside to engage in other activities and returning to it minutes or weeks later. A playgoer may, of course, choose to take a stroll in the lobby in mid-performance but he may miss some necessary question of the play which is then to be considered. If there is no plot development, tension or conflict which compels our interest in the fates of the characters the theatre may quickly be filled with fidgeting, coughing, snoring, or the shuffle of departing feet. The dramatist must know when and how often to build up to and away from climactic moments in his action. The framework on which the dramatist develops his work depends a good deal on strong aural and visual associations built in recognizable patterns. Human beings have, almost from birth, a remarkable capacity to enjoy the complexities of patterns, the repetition of the familiar, and the variations evolving from a familiar base. The comfort we gain from a reliance on the known can be seen in the child's tenacious insistence that his favourite stories be repeated in precise wording without editing and, if possible, with the exact intonation to which he is accustomed. *Avant garde* artists often fight against our reliance on familiar conventions, but the radical experiments they undertake to shake up or shock those with complacent expectations of predictable form and content are quite often absorbed into the mainstream of art as their innovations become familiar enough to give us pleasure in the recognition of pattern. Many formal symmetries and the various techniques which produce structural interconnections can be recognized in the study of a playscript. Such pleasures, however, like the ones to be gained in reading a musical score, are only a preparation for the full apprehension of the strategies of composition which give us such various delights in an actual performance.

Shakespeare often takes it for granted that we know, or think we know, the story he is going to tell us, and he exploits our memories for his own purposes. He also relies heavily on the active participation of our memories within the time-frame of a performance. Scholars have spent a great deal of time naturally enough on the complex structure of verbal echoes in the texts of Shakespeare's plays. By comparison the ways in which the plays use the capacities of our visual memory have received less attention. There are cues in lines of the text and in stage directions which are meant to supply, in the movement and grouping of characters, patterns for our eyes. But these are often perishable because a director can make much of them or ignore them in his individual production. Yet even when a director slashes speeches or scenes from his production there is usually, nowadays at least, enough of the rich, interconnected imagery and pattern of verbal echoes left to give the audience the sense of the organic continuity which is so highly wrought in Shakespeare. Some directors, afflicted with a suburban sensibility, seek to cabin, crib and confine the broad, generous, human rhythms of Shakespeare's plays by turning his work into a 'relevant', polemical commentary on contemporary issues or into a demonstration of current neuroses. With the inflection of the voice or with the aid of visual cues it is possible to impose any kind of eccentric or absurd interpretation on a Shakespeare play. The plays, however, like Proteus resist strenuously all attempts to wrestle them into a straitjacket.

A good director of a Shakespeare play is not trying to be a ventriloquist operating a dummy; he is happy enough to be the dummy himself, to let the play speak through his ability to catch and activate its rhythms. There are a multitude of factors involved in mounting a successful, modern production of a Shakespeare play. Huge sums of money spent on costumes, sets, lighting and properties are no guarantee of success. It remains true that a modest attempt by good amateur actors may strike us as a more successful realization of Shakespeare's intentions than the most ambitious, star-studded performance in one of the world's theatre meccas. Shakespeare had a very exact knowledge of how to make a play work on an audience which is why, quite often, in spite of poor acting, eccentric interpretation and clumsy direction some of the scenes in a production may still move an audience considerably. The plays are not foolproof, but there are so many things going on in a Shakespeare play that it is difficult to knock the shine off all of them at the same time.

The greatest losses an audience must put up with in a production of a badly mangled or heavily cut text are not the missing poetic jewels, the 'ideas', or the absence of subtle grace notes in the characterization, but the structure and shape of the play which communicates itself in the extraordinary precision of its proportions. When a production succeeds in giving us a deeply satisfying experience it is not often the result of a single, bravura acting performance by a star. The plays may, to a degree, be 'star vehicles' but they are made for ensemble acting in very well balanced repertory companies. Success comes from the detailed attention we can sense has been given to each part of the play though we may not be able to describe all the effects. Good verse speaking is important but that music alone will not carry the play. A good production must catch the natural stride of the play as it unfolds in the two- to three-hour traffic of the stage. The director must transmit to the audience the precision and justness in the weighting and proportion within the various parts of the action. He must give us the sense of rightness in the momentum as the pattern of interrelated actions complete themselves. To achieve this all of the verbal echoes have to be used and the visual impact, in the physical movement and grouping of the characters, has to serve the detailed patterning which ties the various strands of plot together.

It may seem obvious enough that a production must strive to reflect the emphases of the play but any experienced playgoer knows that one does not in practice have such an experience as frequently as one might wish. The explanation is not hard to find. For three hundred years and more actors and directors have been judged by their success or failure in coping with Shakespeare. They have undertaken every possible strategy in seeking to avoid failure – they have cut the plays, excised characters, axed whole plots, rewritten them, placed them in every conceivable historical setting, modernized them, marmorealized them, and tried to make them echo every quirky theory of human behaviour and social organization. Despite major surgery, transplants, amputations, and cosmetic modifications the body of the plays endures. Fortunately, because the plays have always attracted the greatest talents in the theatre, there have been triumphant productions and performances which have kept vividly alive the full impact of the plays. The plays are so indelibly marked that their nature cannot be completely stamped out. They have a quality which Olivia claimed for her face. ' 'Tis in grain, sir; 'twill endure wind and weather.' The meaning she is applying is 'dyed in grain' from a French usage 'en graine' which means 'dyed scarlet or crimson, fast dyed'. The word was used also as a predicate, 'indelible, ineradicable' from which the word 'ingrained' developed. It is this fixed, inward quality which Gertrude seemed to discover when she saw in her soul dyed with guilt 'Such black and grained spots/As will not leave their tinct'. The aspects of play structure I am concerned with in this study make another meaning of 'grain' relevant – 'the longitudinal arrangement of fibres or particles, in lines or veins more or less parallel along which the material is more easily cloven or cut than in any other direction, as in wood, producing often the effect of pattern' – a meaning which first appears in the mid-sixteenth century. In these studies I am trying to indicate the grain in the structure of Shakespeare's plays. Shakespeare developed a great variety of strategies to ensure coherence and organic unity in his plays. I have examined two of the strategies on which Shakespeare habitually relied in order to show the ingenious variety of ways in which he exploited them.

The first half of this book is devoted to an analysis of Shakespeare's uses of repetition, echo, pattern and variation within pattern in the organization of the events in his plots. At the simplest level the repetition of a gesture at key emotional climaxes of a play can illuminate an audience's understanding of the development of the action. It often happens that Shakespeare produces scenic structures with corresponding sequences of events between the same or similar characters at different points of the play. Besides the specifically recognizable scenic patterns there are also broader rhythms of action repeated and varied which reinforce our general sense of the action being worked out in two, three or four related movements.

The proscenium arch stage with its back drops, elaborate scenery and curtains leant itself readily to productions which broke up the action and emphasized changes from one locale to another. It was much easier to chop up and reassemble the plays and to regard Shakespeare as a writer of sprawling, cumbersome, imperfectly controlled plots marred by vulgar passages, as someone very much in need of 'improvement', as long as his plays were not performed on the kind of stage for which they were expressly written. As long as scenery was a significant, even dominant, part of the plays' effects then directors tended to think in terms of a visual variety which stemmed from a designer's portfolio rather than from the structure of the play itself. In the rediscovery of the bare, thrust stage, however, we have found out what remarkable precision there is in the structural rhythms of the plays. A mosaic of short scenes with varied actions flows swiftly on an unadorned stage and forces us to see much more readily how one plot acts as a comment on another, how the ending of a scene with one set of characters can relate directly to the beginning of the next scene with another set of characters, how the progression in a sequence of events in the building-block segments of interaction in one scene are carefully reflected in a repeated sequence in a later scene. The continuous flow of action which is possible, even inescapable, on the thrust stage tightens up all the links of the plays. The play generates its energy not simply within each scene but in the cumulative effect of several scenes and in the relationships which it is possible to see between widely separated scenes. Without the distraction of scenery we can focus entirely on the characters unfolding their plots in the wooden arena. The thrust stage, though it denies plays many scenic effects, offers, relative to the proscenium arch stage, much greater opportunity of presenting variety in the movement and grouping of characters because of the way the audience is intimately involved in its three-dimensional effect.

Only a few modern directors have mastered the technique of producing Shakespeare's plays effectively on the thrust stage. One of the first lessons a director must learn in coping with such a stage is the danger of pursuing novelty for its own sake. In the limitations of the stage it is possible to spy out advantages. The director who tries to use the thrust stage with relentless ingenuity gives us productions which are eccentrically mannered. The directorial concepts get in the way of Shakespeare's work. Only when the thrust stage is used in a relaxed, unobtrusive manner does it become a perfectly transparent medium which allows us to see the patterns of the play's action. An audience is thus not fobbed off with a director's ideas but is given the genuine pleasure of observing the way that a Shakespeare play works. Shakespeare left no notes for directors and very few detailed stage directions, yet anyone who has ever directed one of his plays knows that the text is crammed with information about how to make it work. The progress of characters in time is embroidered in a pattern of contrasts and parallels, echoes and distortions. A large part of our understanding of the play arises from our awareness of interconnections in the sequence of events. A director's task is to facilitate as much as possible, by clarifying these links, the work which is demanded of an audience.

When a production on a thrust stage yields full satisfaction to an audience it can produce an impact which is akin to the revelation when years of encrusted grime are removed from a great Venetian painting of the dazzling chromaticism of its original colours. We can rely on verbal echoes and clusters of imagery to make many connections which enrich our awareness of the complex texture of the play. Repetition and extension, patterns incorporating change are the endlessly varying forms of so many of the rhetorical figures in which Renaissance writers took delight. Such devices operate on a grand scale in dramatic structures and must be reflected in the rhythm and pace of performance if the audience is to have the full advantage of Shakespeare's care in structuring his plays.

The strategy which I examine in the second half of this study is also concerned with Shakespeare's judicious sense of proportion and balance in the various actions of his plays. Any good dramatist knows that too great a variety of action may satisfy the audience's need for spectacle at the cost of any coherence in the plot or any engagement in the development of the characters. Too limited a variety in the action may produce over-extended sterile debate. In the vast ranges of Elizabethan drama we can observe every kind of failure to achieve a workable balance. Even if we suppose that the original audience may have had a greater appetite for spectacle and for debate than an audience today we know that the writers who were most valued and rewarded were those who, through judicious variety of action, multiplicity within a unified design, could compel the audience to attend to the interwoven fates of many characters. The Elizabethans habitually attended plays with large casts of characters drawn from a broad range of societal classes, organized into several plots, frequently covering events in an extended period of time in widely separated locales. The problem for the dramatists was not how to introduce variety but how to get control of it to produce a coherently focused experience. Shakespeare's pre-eminence in poetic skill and gifts of characterization have never been in question. Only in the present century have we come to appreciate his skills in the techniques of structuring a multi-faceted drama which determinedly ignores the classical unities.

One almost invariably has the sense that Shakespeare knows precisely how long to run a scene, when to change from one piece of action to another, how much to weight each relationship, which characters to use, like Iago, to oppress the audience by their omnipresence, which characters to keep from the audience, which characters to keep apart from each other on the stage, which action to show us, which action to give merely in report. We know that the proportions achieved within a play among the various actions are the result of careful consideration. The weighting of relationships is often significantly altered from those available in the sources. Sometimes, as in *King Lear*, the structure is almost entirely novel because the material for the two plots is taken from two hitherto totally unrelated stories. In presenting us with this variety Shakespeare does not merely submit to the time limitation of drama in his awareness that the more we see of one relationship the less we can see of another; he makes it work to his advantage. Stories harnessed together can amplify their effect on an audience in ways that they might not achieve separately. Human understanding works by recognizing pattern and contrast. Lear's problems and his responses to them are the stuff of epic saga, but we can define them and relate to them more effectively in their parallels with and radical contrast to the experience of Gloucester.

In the infinite variety of his skills Shakespeare has Cleopatra's ability to make hungry where most he satisfies. He does not achieve this, however, by supplying only caviar to the general. There are certain characters who delight us so much with their wit and imagination that we might like to think we could rest forever in their company. After a moment's reflection, however, we realize that our enjoyment is achieved by a complex method. The wit is a jewel the more dazzling when our access to him is limited, the more sharply defined and savoured by contrast with the dullness or outright stupidity of others. Shakespeare scarcely ever, save for a deliberate purpose, allows his characters to suffer from that problem which so many modern politicians and media stars have to cope with – 'overexposure'. We have a sense that matters have been so nicely judged that even his most attractive characters would have less impact if they had been given greater scope to charm us. We can agree that caviar is good in itself, but it is perhaps the better in that we cannot have it every day and because it is not boiled cabbage.

The studies in the second half of this book are devoted to the variety of techniques employed by Shakespeare in structuring the character relationships which the audience experiences. The relative weighting of the relationships is one of the key factors in regulating the audience's responses to the story and Shakespeare's skill is to be understood not only from the characters he brings together on stage but in the way in which he separates characters and limits our experience of them together. The care and deliberation in handling the relationships can be illuminated often by the way that Shakespeare modifies, cuts, or amplifies the relationships available in the sources. The techniques which I am analysing here were often developed to solve problems which were posed by the material in the sources. None of the sources which Shakespeare used was the work of a great writer. The material in the romances, the chronicles, the hack plays, the prose and verse narratives has not been subjected to the rigour of a great artistic imagination, nor in most cases has it been shaped by the practical demands of dramatic performance in a limited time period. Shakespeare's skill lies not simply in his ingenuity and economy in solving problems which the writer of the narrative source did not need or care to consider. The very grain of Shakespeare's work is created in the way he develops consistent strategies to deal with dramatic problems and incorporates them in a coherent structural design for the whole play.

I have attempted in these studies to employ a little of the skills which I value so much in Shakespeare. I have tried not to place play after play on a slab and carve open the anatomy of each one to demonstrate structural devices as repeated formulas. I have been numbed by many studies which make of all the delectable cuts in Shakespeare neat heaps of ground round. Shakespeare did not write according to formulas. It is his flexible and protean application of basic devices which has engaged my attention. So I have tried, like Shakespeare, to avoid supplying my reader with an over-frequent confrontation with precisely the same use of the strategies in each play. I have tried to maintain variety by working from the small-scale to the full-scale deployment of structural strategies, by dealing at times with a pair of scenes or one relationship and at other times with a whole play or a complete network of interactions. A hack writer churns out material according to mechanical formulas which the audience readily recognizes. A great dramatist very frequently uses his craft to conceal the ways he is achieving his effect upon us. There is a grain in Shakespeare's work but it is not an abstract technique which we can codify in specifications in a play-writing manual. Grain, used in the sense of indelible dye or to mean the veins and fibres which reveal structural organization, helps to differentiate the quality of the materials where it appears. We can understand the grain in Shakespeare's work only by responding to the variety of the material in which we find it. The material is the individual play and it is the story and its needs which determines the grain.

To a large extent man rose to pre-eminence on the globe because of his ability to cut into and discover the grain of things, to define the principles of order in the structure of the organic and inorganic world. Creative artists enjoy their ability to construct a coherent order for their work. One of the pleasures we gain in responding to their work comes from our ability to discover the structure which organizes it. Because man has been able to uncover the secret structures of the material world he has been able to develop tools to exploit and dominate it. He endangers himself and others when he fails to respect the nature of the material and its place in a complex environment. Works of art, especially those which require live performance, are vulnerable to abuse by those who cut and snip without any concentrated inquiry into the structure which they are carving.

My analyses, for the most part, follow the unfolding sequence of a play's events because the success of the strategies depends not only on what events Shakespeare chooses to dramatize for the audience but on the order in which he decides to let us experience them. He worked out these strategies to have an effect not on readers of his plays but on people watching and listening to his plays. The echoes and back references, and weighting of interactions, the scenic connections, the placing of major, formal, public scenes, the visual patterns are calculated to have their effect in a two- to three-hour time span. It is of crucial importance that we try to consider the ways that the plays work from the point of view of the 'naive' audience, for those eager patrons of the Globe who had had no access to a printed version before they experienced them on stage. We must define the problems that Shakespeare copes with and remember that his solutions are calculated for the swiftly unfolding sequence of interactions in live performance. I have tried to indicate how Shakespeare's strategies can be understood in terms of brief incidents or whole structures, how they are shaped or exploited according to specific needs in an individual story. It becomes clear how Shakespeare by manipulating the sequence of events produces echoes, surprises and ironies which emerge in the calculated patterns and judiciously weighed proportions of the play. I am trying to indicate some of the wealth of material Shakespeare provides for a director to make the plays work on an audience. In essence I hope to give some sense of why it is important to go with rather than against the grain in Shakespeare.

Part One

1 · 'Look where it comes again'
Pattern and variation in Shakespeare's dramas

There is a self-reflexive quality on many levels to the drama of Shakespeare's age. Shakespeare seems to have counted on the fact that many members of his audience were long-time loyal supporters of his company. It was not merely the time-frame within an individual play which he could capitalize on, he could occasionally use the longer frame of a theatregoer's habits. When Polonius says to Hamlet, before the play-scene, that he has been an actor and, as Julius Caesar, was killed by Brutus in the Capitol, it is possible that there is a specific reference which would have a particular impact for the original audience. The actor playing Polonius may be the same actor who had recently performed as Shakespeare's Julius Caesar talking to Hamlet/Burbage who may have played Brutus in that same production. An actor playing a character who talks about himself as an actor playing a character is not simply routine metadrama. It is especially appropriate at the moment when Hamlet is broaching his trap, trying to come at reality through illusion. The essence of Caesar's murder was the surprise, the fact that even his closest friend Brutus was involved. The play shortly to be performed is a re-enactment of the murder of one brother by another, and its aim is for a nephew to catch his guilty uncle by surprise. A result of the performance will be that Polonius will be taken by surprise and stabbed by Hamlet through the arras. That very man who had enacted Caesar will become once again a capital calf in the brute stabbing by the man who had played Brutus. These ironies and interconnections are not simultaneously activated in the mind of the audience. The important point is that they are potentially there in the general similarity of event. Out of something seemingly innocent a violent shock emerges which proves a turning point to the action. What Caesar had anticipated as a routine ceremony in the Capitol turns out to be his assassination. What Claudius considers an innocent performance to preoccupy his wayward nephew turns out to be a horrifying revelation that his fratricide is not a buried secret. Polonius, we might eventually feel, would be rather aptly cast as Shakespeare's Julius Caesar. He is something of a sententious windbag, rather addicted to his own theories about Hamlet's antic disposition no matter what contrary evidence is available. Like Caesar he does not respond to signals of danger which pose a threat to his life.

It has often been suggested that the original audiences may have gained added insight or ironical references by the juxtaposition of plays in Shakespeare's canon. We may suppose that *Romeo and Juliet* and *A Midsummer Night's Dream*, written in the same period, could have gathered an extra frisson in the refracted lights they cast on each other in performance. There may have been a special pleasure for an audience profoundly moved by the tragic mistakes of the young lovers in Verona watching, in the same period, the mechanicals turning a very similar tragic story into hysterical farce at the Athenian court. Regular supporters of a stable repertory company have a particular insider's pleasure. Attached to any favourite actor's current role are the shadows of his earlier roles. An accomplished actor developing the variety of his talent can count on our knowledge of his career, our expectations that he is ready for a role, or our hopes for a fresh interpretation when he is cast in a way we had not anticipated. Nick Bottom and Francis Flute are given the most abominable verse ever spoken on a stage to express the toils of Pyramus and Thisby. But the audience finds itself distanced a little from the young courtier lovers who are so eager to make smart cracks at the mechanicals' expense even as they forget their own recent absurd endeavours in the Athenian woods. We have no means of knowing which actors played the parts of, say, Egeus, Demetrius and Hermia. But if they had recently played in repertory Capulet, Paris and Juliet then the original audience would have a slight overlay of awareness of the range of torment, from the broadest farce to the deepest tragedy, to which love could bring the young. They can laugh at Pyramus and Thisby and yet cause the audience to remember how heartrending a tragedy can be which results from the impulsive mistakes of young lovers rushing to death on misleading evidence. That one man in his time plays many parts is a conventional habit of thought in this period, but in the patterns of repertory company performance there were always real theatrical circumstances multiplying the commonplace ironies.

There are many structural similarities between *1 Henry IV* and *2 Henry IV*. It is not enough simply to attribute this, as with so many modern movie sequels, to the reliance on the repetition of a commercially successful formula. The elements – the embattled king in his court, the

Boar's Head Tavern revellers, the truant Prince moving from one locale to the other, the disaffected Percies – all recur. There is enough parallelism in some of the scenic structures to make it seem possible that Shakespeare counted on the audience of Part 2 remembering some of the incidents of Part 1. If they were intended to be played again in sequence, as they so often are by modern repertory companies, then the patterning in scenic structures would reinforce the effect of the speeches which recall past kings and battles to create a sense of the cyclic movement of historical events. But the mood and tone of the second part are completely different from those of the first. It seems likely that Shakespeare is using a superficial repetition of pattern, as he does so often, to emphasize change.

In *1 Henry IV* Falstaff is on stage in eight scenes of the play and in all of those scenes he shares the stage at some point with Hal. Hal appears in ten scenes of the play. Falstaff is on stage without Hal for less than 200 lines of the play. Hal is on stage without Falstaff for a little less than 500 lines. They are on stage together for almost 1000 lines, a third of the play, and for nearly all of them they are engaged in direct interaction . In *2 Henry IV* there is a very significant alteration made in the weight given to direct exchanges between the two. Falstaff appears in eight of the play's scenes but in only two of those scenes does he share the stage with Hal. Hal is on stage in only five scenes. Falstaff is on stage in events in which Hal takes no part for over 1200 lines of the play. Hal is on stage in scenes without Falstaff for a little less than 500 lines. But the two characters engage in direct interaction for only around 150 lines, less than one-twentieth of the play. Thus we see Hal and Falstaff together in Part 1 for over six times more lines than in Part 2 and we see Falstaff without Hal for six times more lines in Part 2 than in Part 1. In spite of so much repetition in the elements of the action we notice the separation of Hal and Falstaff and the way in which the plays drive towards totally different conclusions. On the surface the last scenes in each play have a broadly similar event as a focus – the search by Falstaff for reward. The chaos of the battle at Shrewsbury in Part 1 with raging rebels, counterfeit kings and the grinning honour of death provide a patchwork of events in which Falstaff can act the coward, lie down, resurrect himself and claim a reward he has not earned. He is still close enough to Hal for the young Prince to wink at his outrageous effrontery. Though the fat man does not know it, Shrewsbury is the pinnacle of his success with Hal. In writing a second play about Henry IV's reign Shakespeare varies a familiar pattern of events to make it clear that Falstaff is soon going to be edged into the tiring house. He may still have a good deal to say 'in behalf of that Falstaff' but remarkably little of it is to Hal. By the end of Part 2 the realm has long been secured from the rebels at Gaultree. Hal has gone through the trial of his father's death and the awesome burden of assuming the crown. Falstaff has been at his roguish exploits in the countryside far from his Jove. He rushes to London for his reward on hearing of Hal's coronation. He can only do so because he, unlike the audience, notices no change in the pattern of events and the nature of his relationship to Hal. At Shrewsbury he could pretend to have earned a reward; now he expects a reward merely for being himself, a boon companion. Falstaff is unaware that the only remaining action in the play, which will complete Hal's long-promised transformation, is the cold rejection which awaits him. In the darkening mood of Part 2, in the sourness which has crept into the Boar's Head antics, in the sense we have of Hal leaving his pranks behind, everything leads us to this conclusion. We expect it because it completes a pattern worked through the play, but the ruthlessness of the rejection still shocks us. That is partly caused by our awareness that there is enough of the old pattern of events remaining, a pattern in which Falstaff thrived, to sustain his conviction that all the world always has been, is and ever will be 'playing holidays'. I think the effect of the final scene in *2 Henry IV* always gains an added impact for an audience that has recently seen *1 Henry IV*. We remember the promise of banishment ('I do, I will') which Hal made at the Boar's Head when he anticipated the time that his house would have to be put in order. Percy was a factor being fattened up for sacrifice. What Falstaff never understands is that he, too, is merely a factor and he is the first roasted Manningtree ox to be offered up on the altar of responsible kingship.

If it can be accepted from these scattered and diverse examples that Shakespeare used pattern and variation, echoes, contrasts and back references from play to play, then it seems probable that he would take advantage of such structural devices *within* his plays. It is possible to find precisely balanced parts within the symmetrical structure of individual scenes. There are throughout his work several basic techniques of scene building, but whether a scene achieves a symmetry in two, three, five or more segments, a rising crescendo in one unbroken interaction or the intercutting of several diverse elements of character and plot, the design will always serve the larger rhythms which are individually developed within each play. An audience in a theatre is not counting lines, nor does it usually focus on the nature of symmetrical segments as a purely formal pleasure. The director must combine all of the verbal and visual elements of the production so that the audience feels the sure sense of the play's movement.

One of the most obvious ways in which Shakespeare exploits the structural pattern in his scenes is to make us conscious of how events seem to repeat themselves in different parts of a play. The repetition can serve to demonstrate the way in which different characters can respond to events in a similar fashion. A repeated pattern of action can give us a sense of the cyclic nature of events, a technique exploited with ingenious variety in the history plays. At other times Shakespeare can underline deliberate contrasts within a recognizably repeated pattern of events so that the audience can focus on the change in fortunes or absorb more fully the shock of realizing how many things have changed since the characters first appeared. I will start out with some simple incidents within widely separated scenes used as echoes, then move on to the repetition of action in scenes of complex organization, and indicate finally how such repeating patterns can be used as the key elements in the total framework on which the action of the play is based. My argument starts with gestures or brief flashes of action which a good director uses to make an audience attend to continuity and change within the lives of the characters. It proceeds to scenes in which the repeating pattern is so obvious that the audience cannot avoid considering the significance of the connection. There are, however, deeper and broader parallels in the structural organization of events which do not depend for their effect on the audience's awareness of the echo of a specific incident or interaction. The director can use such patterns not for a momentary effect but as a way of orchestrating the tempo and rhythm of the action of the whole play. It is of crucial importance that all of these elements which reveal the grain of a play's structure be given their appropriate emphasis to provide an audience with a coherent production.

In a straightforward example from *King Lear* we can see the way one scene links back to another and illuminates for us the process of change in character. In II. iv Lear is involved, to his own surprise, in the repetition of an earlier action. The Fool knew, of course, that the humiliating lesson Goneril had taught Lear would be given again: 'Shalt see thy other daughter will use thee kindly; for though she's as like this as a crab's like an apple, yet I can tell what I can tell' (I. v. 12–14). Before Lear arrives the audience already knows that Regan intends to strip him further of his illusions of power. Why, we may ask, does Shakespeare devote so much stage time to Regan's reprise of Goneril's lesson to Lear about the new facts of life regarding the disposition of power in his kingdom? Shakespeare made a fundamental alteration of his source-story when he decided that Lear must be driven to madness by his misfortunes. Lear must, therefore, be exposed to unrelenting pressure as both of his daughters attempt to wrestle his power from him. The confrontation with Regan disabuses Lear of the illusion that he can make a better bargain. The audience must see that Lear is so imbued with autocratic stubbornness that he refuses to learn a lesson even though it is taught to him twice. The daughters want to humiliate him into docile, doddering dependency, but his fury and his curses grow in extravagance until he storms out on to the heath. We can see how far he is from humility in a key moment, which has great visual impact, when he scornfully parodies the obsequiousness his daughters seem to expect of him. He puts on a role, or does an audition for it, to indicate how inappropriate it is:

REGAN: . . . . Therefore I pray you
That to our sister you do make return;
Say you have wronged her.
LEAR: Ask her forgiveness?
Do you but mark how this becomes the house:
'Dear daughter, I confess that I am old.
[*Kneels*]
Age is unnecessary. On my knees I beg
That you'll vouchsafe me raiment, bed, and food.'
REGAN: Good sir, no more. These are unsightly tricks.
Return you to my sister.
LEAR: [*Rises*]   Never, Regan.

                         (II. iv. 145–53)

In acting the role of beggar he hopes to shame Regan into allowing him to continue in his role as imperious monarch. His satirical performance, though he knows it not, is a prescient anticipation of the road he will take. He will explore the art of our necessities, he will meet beggars and try to identify with them. He will strip off his raiment, be denied his bed and forego food. This specialist in the elaborate rhetorical thunder of cursing who could only use the simple language of a helpless old man as a jest moves steadily towards a turning point. The whole process of the play brings Lear to his knees, moves him from mock humility to genuine humility.

In IV. vii Lear is reunited with the daughter he had banished. He acknowledges the injustice of his actions and seeks forgiveness from Cordelia. Shakespeare reminds us of the distance he has travelled by making him act, with heart rending sincerity, the role he had once so contemptuously mocked:

LEAR: . . . . I know not what to say.
      I will not swear these are my hands. Let's see –
      I feel this pin prick. Would I were assured
      Of my condition.
CORDELIA: O look upon me, sir,
      And hold your hand in benediction o'er me.
You must not kneel.
LEAR: Pray, do not mock me.
      I am a very foolish fond old man,
      Fourscore and upward, not an hour more nor less;
      And, to deal plainly,
      I fear I am not in my perfect mind.

                                       (IV. vii. 54–63)

There are many ways in which this moment can be acted. I have seen Cordelias who move swiftly enough to prevent Lear from doing anything more than simply sketching in the crook of a knee. I have seen Lears who have knelt down for ten, even fifteen lines of this climactic exchange, resisting all attempts to help them stand up. Since the moment is set up quite deliberately in reflection of that earlier sequence at Regan's, it is important to block the stage movements so that the audience gets the flash of recognition. That, in my view, involves having Lear kneel down to Cordelia. The great advantage of the bare, thrust stage is that it lends itself easily to such visual back-reference. A good director will have Lear kneel in the same place on stage as he had done before and he will put Cordelia in the position that Regan had occupied. The play is overlaying one visual image on another and the slight clues ensure that the audience makes the connection. The plays offer many such opportunities for visual cross-reference. This sequence has one more final touch of verbal embroidery when Lear and Cordelia have been captured in battle. Lear asks for nothing more than a life in prison with Cordelia:

No, no, no, no! Come, let's away to prison.
We two alone will sing like birds i' th' cage.
When thou dost ask me blessing, I'll kneel down
And ask of thee forgiveness.

                                        (V. iii. 8–11)

Lear had demanded that all of his daughters beg his blessing in the division of his realm. At that time he could never have imagined himself kneeling in sincere humility to beg a blessing of any of them. But this unaccommodated old man eventually finds that he could happily make a career of kneeling down. The act of kneeling down which is allowed to him, though not signalled in the text, is one which most directors supply – the crushed and huddled figure bending over his daughter's lifeless body in the final moments of the play.

Such vivid signals of the interconnectedness of the elements of a story have a poweful impact in their direct simplicity. Shakespeare uses the kneeling down of characters in several of his plays and on the bare boards of the thrust stage such an action registers with memorable effect. We are clearly meant to connect two sequences of kneeling for purposes of contrast in *Othello*. When the Moor is completely convinced that he is a cuckold he asserts an icy determination to sweep to his revenge. He kneels down to swear a vow by heaven that he will not be satisfied until he has accomplished his aim. In a sickening moment of extreme cynicism Iago prevents Othello from rising and, kneeling at his side, swears something akin to an oath of blood-brotherhood in serving the cause of revenge. The sequence affirms a bond in prayer in the shared task of resolving Othello's torment by killing Cassio and Desdemona (III. iii. 453–80). Only a few scenes later, at the end of the brothel scene, we see Desdemona convinced at last that her husband suspects her of unfaithfulness. She turns to Iago for help and advice about how 'to win my lord again'. Then she kneels and swears by the constancy of her love that she will always love Othello no matter what treatment she receives at his hands (IV. ii. 148–61). Iago does not, of course, kneel and swear a bond with Desdemona, but his presence on both occasions when husband and then wife turn to him for help makes the connection. In the declarations of constancy, in the bold rhetoric which exhibits unquestioning confidence in their own decisions, the one to murder, the other to love come what may, we feel a link between the two passages. The director can help to press upon us the ghoulish nature of the contrast in these bonds of faith by having Desdemona kneel in the same place Othello had done, and by having Iago's movements and attitude as far as possible underline the correspondence of the sequences. I would myself have Iago kneel down beside her in sympathy as he helps her to her feet (IV. ii. 165–7).

Shakespeare often presents not merely an incident but a whole scene with the same general structural pattern to act as an echo of a scene we have witnessed earlier, but by making variations in the pattern he emphasizes the changes wrought by time. One of the clearest examples of his technique is the development of the two scenes in *Measure for Measure* where Isabella pleads with Angelo for her brother's life. The plot has no specific logistical problems which require that there should be two separate interviews. Shakespeare's method of showing two phases in Angelo's submission to his sensual impulses does, however, serve the psychological needs of his audience. He uses the interval between the two scenes to bring the disguised Duke, after an absence of several scenes, back to the centre of the action. His return is reassuring to the audience at precisely the moment we see Isabella moving into danger, and Angelo, as the Duke had anticipated, beginning to crumble. Angelo's reputation and behaviour have impressed upon us his 'snow-broth' nature. It was not beyond the skills of Shakespeare to dramatize the collapse of such a nature into sensuality in one continuous scene. The Duke has hinted, and Angelo's own behaviour has led us to expect, that we are in a situation where 'pride goeth before a fall'. But the transformation which we are to observe is not confined to Angelo. We observe the cold, restrained nature of Isabella (II. ii) slowly warming to her task. We eventually have to see her (II. iv) repelled by the grossness of Angelo's suggestions. We have to absorb the full impact of this affront to Isabella if we are to understand her behaviour later with Claudio. We meet Isabella on the doorstep of a convent about to cloister herself from any of the normal interactions between the sexes. To thaw Isabella and to turn her into a pure flame of argument Shakespeare used Lucio as a catalyst. She is not the kind of person so convinced of her mission that she would visit Angelo alone in order to argue her case. But if Angelo is to reveal the flame of passion which is consuming him then it cannot be done in the presence of other witnesses. It would have been possible, perhaps, to send Lucio and the Provost off stage, leaving Angelo to pursue the path of periphrases to the eventual direct declarations of his lust. Shakespeare is concerned not only with the effects of Angelo's fall but also with its process. One of the major advantages he can exploit by breaking this sequence of action into two scenes is to give the audience detailed insight into Angelo's own horror and amazement at his susceptibility to lust in the soliloquies which he places after the first interview and before the second one (II. ii. 162–87; II. iv. 1–17, 19–30). The audience must not be allowed to sit back in smug satisfaction at Angelo's faltering, it must see something of his suffering. The experience we have of this proud man trying to accommodate new sensations helps to explain how he comes to play such a hypocritical game in reneging on the bargain he makes with Isabella. The difference between the tone of the two soliloquies is a key example of how Shakespeare could create the impression of the change which many hours have wrought in a few minutes of elapsed stage time. The Angelo who reels in shocked surprise at the very idea that he can even contemplate committing a sin gives place to the man who has spent hours praying unsuccessfully for the strength to resist temptation and who is on the verge of allowing the tide of sensuality to take him whatever way it chooses.

In structure the scene which culminates in the first soliloquy and the scene which develops out of the second one have a good deal in common.

Act II, Scene ii

(i)   In the preparation for the central section of the scene we have a preliminary appeal from the Provost on Claudio's behalf. Angelo's rejection of this appeal reaffirms the sternness of his stance up to the very instant that temptation is to begin undoing his resolve. 1–25.

(ii)   Isabella builds up her case in a series of speeches presented initially with a coldness which Angelo easily brushes aside, but ultimately argued with a zealous urgency that unsettles him. 25–161.

(iii)   Angelo, in soliloquy, reveals the havoc Isabella has wrought. 161–87.

The whole scene in its build-up to and away from Isabella's powerful arguments has something of the quality of a siege of a sturdy castle. Between the conclusion of this scene and the opening of II. iv we have only the forty-two lines of the Duke's talk with Juliet. The second interview has precisely the same number of lines as the first one. It has an introductory section, a central interaction and a concluding soliloquy of reaction in roughly the same weighted proportions as before.

Act II, Scene iv

(i)   Angelo, in soliloquy, is horrified by the uncontrollable 'swelling evil' within him. 1–30.

(ii)   While Isabella makes her arguments for Claudio's release Angelo moves from innuendo to open declarations of his determination to satisfy his lust. 30–170.

(iii)   Isabella, in soliloquy, acknowledges that she cannot publicly shame Angelo but she determines not to submit to any private shame herself. 171–87.

On the surface both of the characters seem to be repeating a debate about sin and mercy, but the audience notices a radical change in the tactics of the debaters. Our focus in the first scene is initially on Isabella and how she has to be warmed up to articulate an effective argument. But the more eloquent she becomes the more we attend to the devastating effect she is having on Angelo. The focus in the second scene is initially on the ravaged Angelo and his futile attempts to keep his hot desires within the bounds of delicate suggestion, but gradually the focus turns to the effect of the revelation of Angelo's lust on Isabella. In the first scene there is a propriety and formality about the debate as Lucio and the Provost add asides of encouragement which give the audience the key as to how Isabella gradually finds 'the vein'. But there is no such distancing effect, no audience on stage filtering events in the second scene. The sense of danger is accentuated not only by the passionate revelations in Angelo's soliloquies but also because Isabella has to confront the deputy alone. In such circumstances, without fear of discovery, Angelo can speak 'more gross' and give his 'sensual race the rein'. Angelo has no leisure now to be dazzled by pearls of wisdom. The impatience of the sensual man gives the scene a jerky and frenetic urgency. Isabella only gradually comes to realize that she is the one under siege. All of the superficial similarities, all of the repetitions in the framing of the scenes, enable us to see the more clearly the different pictures they contain. The simplest way of calculating the change in emphasis is to note how in the central debate section of each scene the relative weighting of the parts varies. In II. ii Isabella speaks some eighty-five lines while Angelo speaks less than forty lines. In II. iv Isabella has about sixty lines while Angelo has over eighty lines. In the first scene we observe how Isabella's behaviour produces a complete transformation in Angelo, until he finds himself alone almost incapable of coping with a new awareness of himself. In the second scene the new Angelo slowly reveals himself but he produces no metamorphosis in Isabella. Instead the resistance to sin, which has crumbled in him, becomes the more strongly affirmed in her as she determines to preserve her chastity.

The device of presenting two versions of a basically similar event is found in the parallel sequences of the gulling of Benedick and Beatrice in *Much Ado About Nothing*. The repetition of scenic structure in these two 'eavesdropping' scenes is quite deliberate and much of the fun arises from our observation of how these two proud figures can be taken in by the same easy device. An outline of the segments of action in each scene reveals the importance of variation within the pattern.

Act II, Scene iii

(i)   After sending his boy for a book Benedick, in soliloquy, speaks mockingly of the qualities he will demand in a woman before he could consider marriage. Typically Shakespeare presents his character firmly assured of himself on the threshold of a major change. 1–32.

(ii)   When those intent on gulling him enter Benedick retires into an arbour. They do not proceed directly with their device but listen first to a song from Balthazar on the fickleness of men – an apt prologue to their theme. 33–86.

(iii)   Pedro, Leonato and Claudio speak of Beatrice's love for Benedick. They bait the hook well and the fish bites. 87–201.

(iv)   After their departure Benedick, in soliloquy, revises his opinion of marriage. 202–25.

(v)   Beatrice arrives to summon Benedick to dinner and from her cool behaviour he manages, nevertheless, to interpret signs which confirm his belief in the passion he has heard of while in hiding. 226–42.

The scene has a rough balance of lines in a symmetrical structure building up in two segments to a central sequence, and developing out of it two short segments of the immediate consequences.

(i)	(ii)	(iii)	(iv)	(v)
32	54	115	24	17

Benedick is presented as seeming simply to 'happen' on the conversation. It is made clear at the mid-point of the scene (115–18) that he has taken the bait. Imagery about snaring birds and fish continues in III. i.

Act III, Scene i

Shakespeare cleverly concluded the gulling of Benedick with a demonstration of Beatrice's irritation at him. He required, therefore, no prologue in which the victim demonstrates a proud and disdainful resistance to the charms of the opposite sex at the moment the trap was about to be sprung. Beatrice is set up rather more deliberately than Benedick and she comes with the intention of eavesdropping.

(i)   Hero sends Margaret to fetch Beatrice and then, with Ursula, sets up the plot to gull the 'lapwing'. 1–23.

(ii)   Hero and Ursula, as soon as their victim enters, speak of Benedick's passion and of Beatrice's disdainful nature. 24–106.

(iii)   Beatrice, left alone, stung by the criticism of her proud, scornful nature, indicates she will requite Benedick's love. 107–16.

This provides a symmetrical division of lines.

(i)	(ii)	(iii)
23	83	10

The build up in the first gulling, with the initial soliloquy and the musicians, is more elaborate. There the double focus – those conducting the gulling and the victim in hiding – is much more clearly stressed. Benedick is given two 'asides' before the gulling proper begins. We hear him speak two 'asides' as the initial snare is laid which indicate that he is falling into the trap. And the male conspirators are given several 'asides' as their game progresses. In the second scene, however, the women only make comment on their victim at the outset and at the conclusion. Beatrice is given no 'asides' to cue an audience to her reactions. The actress playing Beatrice must rely on facial expression and gesture to indicate that she is taking the bait. The focus of attack also differs quite markedly in the two scenes. The emphasis in the argument of the men is on the desperate state of the lovelorn Beatrice. There is comparatively little space devoted to the cruelty of Benedick's pride. So the male ego is flattered in hearing of the havoc it has caused, and is encouraged to take pity on a lady in despair. The women, in laying their snares, focus not so much on Benedick's love-tormented condition as on Beatrice's scornful nature and on the handsome, virtuous nature of the man she so persistently disdains.

The second scene is less than half the length of the first gulling because with the basic pattern established a shorthand version that has all the essentials will suffice. There is no assurance in 'asides' that Beatrice is swallowing the bait because we assume that she is as vulnerable as Benedick. This is as clear an example as one could wish of Shakespeare's knowledge of how much is enough. Much of our laughter rises from the repetition. But the gulling of Beatrice is, quite deliberately, not as amusing as that of Benedick. Shakespeare knew how much fun he could expect to get out of a twice-told joke. By slight variations and by economy he extracts much more than he would ever get by wearying the audience with a complete repetition. Why, then, we may ask, does Shakespeare make Benedick rather than Beatrice the victim of the more elaborate gulling? It is consonant with his aim from the outset to emphasize the unnaturalness of Benedick's resistance to love and marriage. His disdain for women, his determination to remain a bachelor, his mockery of those winged by Cupid is much more prominently presented than the disdain we find in the behaviour of Beatrice. The proportions in the gulling of the lovers and in the ways they make fools of themselves are in a very just ratio. We can enjoy watching Benedick take the bait, we can smile at his comments as he becomes more firmly hooked, we can roar with laughter as, Malvolio-like, he twists signs of affection out of near-insults precisely because he was so cockily confident when he entered this very scene that he was invulnerable to love's dart. Beatrice has to be brought down from her high horse with substantially less glee because we are never completely convinced she is happy to be up there in the first place. From her first inquiries about Signor Mountanto we suspect that her scorn may be a cover for an attraction to Benedick. We perceive that he is the hunted one and that Beatrice's barbs are revenge for Benedick's rejection of her in earlier encounters. She may have ventured once for Benedick and failed and so the defensive scorn resulting from a wound to her pride may have rather more substance than Benedick's misogyny. Benedick is, after all, a public campaigner against love. Young Claudio in love is the butt of his wit. Beatrice's barbs, however, are reserved mainly for Benedick. And even though she rails against husbands her healthy enjoyment of Hero's success in love indicates that she does not seriously embrace a general philosophy that all men are to be rejected or that marriage is to be avoided at all costs.

In his cycles of history plays Shakespeare developed a habit of weaving diverse material together by the use of ironical anticipation in prophecy and the retrospective summary of events. The repeated and extended pattern of the clash of mighty households and the rise and fall of kings is outlined within plays and across the sequences of plays. Beyond these more general linkages there are specific scenes which emphasize a repetition in a pattern of events. In two scenes in *Richard III* every audience is obliged to recognize Gloucester's sinister method of undermining his victims: the wooing of Lady Anne (I. ii) and its reprise in the assault on Queen Elizabeth for the hand of her daughter (IV. iv). These scenes may have been suggested by the two wooing scenes in Legge's *Richardus Tertius* or by hints taken from Seneca's *Hercules Furens*. The scenes in Legge do not involve the same women but they do present the victims pouring invective on a butcher who woos them in spite of the fact that he has slaughtered their relatives. The idea of developing detailed structural correspondences between the scenes is attributable solely to Shakespeare.

The assault on Lady Anne vividly establishes for an audience the techniques of a man who is willing to violate ceremony, decorum, every civilized standard of behaviour in his ruthless pursuit of power. Everything about this disturbing scene is designed to emphasize Richard's unnaturalness. The audience can only gasp at the deformed prince's audacity in wooing Anne amid the obsequies for the anointed king, her father-in-law, whom Richard has recently murdered. In the inventive use of a detail in Holinshed Shakespeare brings even the corpse of Henry VI in the coffin as close as it can come to a gasp by having its wounds bleed afresh. Anne asks for the aid of God, of earth, of heaven, of lightning to kill the butcher who torments her. We have here, as throughout the play, references which recall the schematized opposition of good angels and devils so common in medieval drama. But the aid of good angels is not readily available and Anne must cope with the demon as best she can. The appalling process of the seduction of Anne is given an extra edge by having the coffin remain on stage until she departs. Henry VI remains as a kind of mute witness while Gloucester goes to hideous lengths to further his own move towards the crown. Any good director will make this coffin something like a net over which the match of wooing is played. If Anne contrives to forget the crimes against her the audience cannot. She enters as a mourner and exists as something close to the affianced bride of the devil she had so recently spurned. The whole scene has the vivid quality of a siege wherein the castle, which had at first seemed invulnerable, is breached as a result of incessant assault. In breaking down the scene into the component elements of a siege we can see how Shakespeare lays down a pattern which he repeats and varies later in the play.

Act I, Scene ii

(i)   Anne recounts her griefs over the coffin of her dead husband's father, Henry VI, and curses Richard, the murderer of both, by wishing that he may have a wife more miserable than she is herself. 1–32.

(ii)   Upon Richard's interruption of the funeral procession we have some preliminary skirmishing as Anne recounts the losses she has suffered at his hands and vents her spleen upon him. 33–111.

(iii) Richard makes his first assault when he suggests Anne should share his bedchamber. When she counters with more accusations he claims that it was her beauty which led him to crime. Through wordplay she deliberately misunderstands his drift. 112–37.

(iv) Richard moves to an open declaration of his intention to be her husband. 138–45.

(v) She begins her first repulse by spitting at him. 146–50.

(vi) He proceeds in his attack by reminding her that all his sins were for her sake and declares that he is willing to balance the books by offering his breast in sacrifice to the sword he places in her hand. 151–82.

(vii) When she lets the sword fall Anne yields ground and thus prepares to submit. 183–98.

(viii) She capitulates completely when she accepts Richard's ring and is sent off to await his pleasure. 199–224.

(ix) Richard comments in soliloquy on his triumph. 227–63.

The scene thus weaves together a series of scornful but ever weakening defensive postures with the mounting of ever more ingeniously audacious assaults. The soliloquy which closes the scene contains an outrageous reversal. Richard who has wooed a widow on her way to a funeral now finds her behaviour unseemly. His cock-crowing triumph asserts how gallant and brave her husband was and how indecorous it is in her to submit to his murderer. Some people have, so it seems, no sense of propriety.

One might expect that a dramatist who wishes to convince an audience of Richard's ability to persuade a woman he had widowed to marry him would go to work carefully and slowly. It might be wise to broach the proposal in one scene, develop the relationship in another, and present the woman's capitulation later on. Shakespeare decides otherwise. Like a magician he brings off the whole trick before our very eyes in one continuous 260-line confrontation. The magical audacity that Shakespeare uses attaches itself to Richard. The trick of any magician is the more effective the more the audience is prepared to believe it is impossible. If Shakespeare had devoted proportionally more of his play to this action it would have less of an impact. The breathtaking economy has a number of supplementary benefits for the play as a whole. It dazzles us with Richard's insolence, his wit, his hypnotic ascendancy, his taste for melodramatic gesture, his impatience and the ruthless speed that mark all of his triumphs. The scene has the effect of an inoculation; after experiencing his success here we do not anticipate any obstacles in his later manoeuvres. By achieving all this in one brief sweep of action Shakespeare leaves himself the more space to unfold all the various stratagems which Richard employs in compassing the crown. Richard is not characterized as a manipulator of devious and clever plots. It is the transparent lack of complexity in his evil actions that is breathtaking. In everyone's eyes he is a deformed hedgehog and most people either call him a villain or have little doubt that he is one. In this society such an amoral, aristocratic nature can succeed in a relentless, impatient drive for power. Anne Neville feels the blowtorch of Richard's complete attention for the fifteen or so minutes that it takes her to capitulate. For the rest of her life she is ignored. The comment that the cynical Richard makes, 'I'll have her, but I will not keep her long,' applies in a different sense to Shakespeare's employment of Anne. In his art Shakespeare has a good deal of the ruthlessness with which he endowed Richard. Characters are brought to life for as long as they are needed. If they threaten to get in the way they are bumped off. By never presenting her again with Richard after the initial wooing, he reminds us of how marginal a figure she is. Anne is brought on stage only once more (IV. i) quite simply to remind us that his unhappy queen is still alive just before Richard begins shopping for a replacement. Anne merely confirms her helplessness which Shakespeare has prepared his audience to accept by the simple device of keeping her off the stage for so long.

In IV. iv there is a long prologue to the siege of Queen Elizabeth in which a group of forlorn women recount their losses, share their griefs, and define their powerless vulnerability. Like Anne they have been stripped by Richard of their kin, as Queen Margaret's catalogue indicates:

> I had an Edward, till a Richard killed him;
> I had a Harry, till a Richard killed him:
> Thou hadst an Edward, till a Richard killed him;
> Thou hadst a Richard, till a Richard killed him. (IV. iv. 40–3)

Margaret identifies Richard as a hound of hell just as Anne had done earlier. The lamentation continues in a detailed recollection of an earlier scene (I, iii) when Margaret had prophesied precisely this state of affairs:

QUEEN ELIZABETH:
O, thou didst prophesy the time would come

> That I should wish for thee to help me curse
> That bottled spider, that foul bunch-backed toad!
>
> QUEEN MARGARET:
> I called thee then vain flourish of my fortune;
> I called thee then poor shadow, painted queen,
> The presentation of but what I was .. . . (IV. iv. 79–84)

The exchange takes us back to the moment when Richard began to reach for the crown and, by association, to the seduction of Lady Anne, a scene which is to be played again in a few moments in a key slightly altered. Margaret reminds Elizabeth that she has already lost most of her kin in this struggle (92–113). In this mirror of her declining fortunes Elizabeth is made to recognize what she once was and what she now is. But she is not yet quite as marginal a figure as Margaret. She has remaining kin who can be exploited by Gloucester. Shakespeare stacks the odds against Richard for, immediately before his entrance, Elizabeth is presented, as Lady Anne was, in a mood as unreceptive as one can imagine for his proposal.

Richard enters to woo Elizabeth by proxy for her daughter as a replacement for the Anne he had earlier wooed in a like manner. The ground has been so well prepared that we have no doubts that Richard will succeed in his aim. The sense of *déjà vu* we experience in recognizing the familiar pattern of assault forces us to concentrate on the confident ease with which Richard manipulates his victim. To a certain degree an audience is surprised and may even enjoy Richard's sprightly insolence in wooing Lady Anne. But the play documents how the practice of evil becomes a routine. Shakespeare is not yet the master-dramatist who could present so economically Macbeth's weariness at the banal repetition of crimes to which his course has condemned him. But already he has caught the cynicism of the criminal mind which pursues its stratagems with a kind of repetitive, mechanical expertise. With Anne we were stunned by the novelty of his tactics, with Elizabeth we are inured to their predictability.

Shakespeare devotes almost the same number of lines to the seduction of Queen Elizabeth – 234 (IV. iv. 197–430) – as he had given to the wooing of Lady Anne (I. ii. 1–224). The scenes begin with the same violent accusations of the losses sustained in the murder of kin. There are the same strategies of wordplay as the antagonists pick up each other's phrases and turn them against their opponent. With only slight variation the same pattern of assault and repulse is played out.

Act IV, Scene iv

(i)   In the initial skirmishing Elizabeth concentrates on the losses of her sons and asserts that she will go to any extreme to avoid further losses. 197–235.

(ii)   Richard moves in periphrastic suggestions towards his proposal. 236–55.

(iii)   Richard makes an open declaration of his intent and Elizabeth, with a play on words, mocks his suggestion. 256–64.

(iv)   Elizabeth mounts her first defence by mocking the absurdity of a lover wooing one whose kin he has slain. 265–90.

(v)   Richard makes his second assault, asserting that he will make up for past injuries by present benefits – his method of balancing the ledger. His bribes are the promise of grandchildren to replace the children Elizabeth has lost. To replace a son who would have been king Elizabeth can have a daughter who will be queen. Dorset will be allowed to return from abroad and will be given promotion. 291–336.

(vi)   Elizabeth makes a second defence with her continuing scorn. But, as with Anne, the stichomythia and barbed wordplay indicate increasing desperation, a preparation for the transition to capitulation. In staying to bandy insults she dallies with temptation. 337–96.

(vii)   Richard makes his third assault by insisting that their happiness and the stability of the realm depend on her willingness to submit to his request. 397–417.

(viii)   Elizabeth now openly falters. Even as she recalls her injuries she considers acquiescence. 418–25.

(ix)   She capitulates completely and is despatched to her task. 426–30.

(x)   The triumphant Richard reflects on his victory (431) and then moves on immediately to other business for the remainder of the scene.

In the earlier scene Richard had been so delighted, even surprised, at his success that he had devoted thirty-four lines of soliloquy to his reactions. But now the practised villain gives one contemptuous line of reaction to his success: 'Relenting fool, and shallow, changing woman!' Though the process has been much the same the effect is different. The earlier scene is a unit, a showpiece of his skill. The second sequence is only an interlude in a larger flow of events – less than half of a huge

538-line scene. In the first scene we have the direct shock of the woman herself yielding to seduction. In the second Richard works indirectly through the mother and moves on to more pressing matters. This reprise of a scenic structure is not an example of self-indulgence in Shakespeare's art. It functions effectively as a way of impressing on the audience his view of Richard's opportunistic nature. In the second scene we are obliged to accommodate ourselves to a sickening and uncomfortable sense of inevitability in events. It is precisely this feeling of inevitability which explains Richard's ascendancy over his victims within the play and his audience outside it. No matter what evidence accumulates against him Richard moves onwards to the crown. He succeeds not merely because of his ruthlessness but because his victims, knowing that he cannot be trusted with an inch of rope, nevertheless give to him the several yards he requires in order to hang them. It is not reasonable that a woman can spit on a man one minute and think of marrying him the next, but it happens. Shakespeare's view of evil grew in complexity but he never abandoned the view that the villain succeeds, in part, because his victims refuse to act on the evidence staring them in the face. The political circumstances of Lady Anne and Queen Elizabeth vary considerably in detail, yet a very similar pattern of seduction works with both of them. There has been a massive accumulation of evidence since the first seduction in the string of victims Richard has exploited. They do not, however, serve as an effective warning to Elizabeth. Shakespeare thus emphasizes how the tyrant holds sway as long as his enemies fail to act in their common cause and for the good of the country and choose rather to pursue illusory personal profits.

There are correspondences and contrasts in the plays of a more elaborate nature than the echoing of recognizably similar events. There are in the build up of climactic sequences, at widely separated points in a play, underlying rhythms which can make an audience feel a significant relationship between events. *Hamlet* is organized in two very long sequences of action which move, though by very devious ways, to a climax of public confrontation between Claudius and the Prince, the mighty opposites of the action. From the point of the Ghost's appearance at the outset all of the action is related to two urgent searches for certain knowledge – Hamlet's need to know if the Ghost is honest, Claudius's need to know the cause and real nature of Hamlet's antic disposition. Everything leads to Hamlet's test in the play-within-the-play. The only character we have met up to this point who is not present at the play is Laertes. The play, in an exciting crescendo, reaches a turning point and an impasse. The moment Hamlet resolves his own uncertainty Claudius is able to do the same. Thus the action builds up again in a long rolling wave to the moment when the two characters, who had discovered the danger each poses for the other in the middle of the play, take their final pass at acting on the knowledge they had then acquired. The play is for any audience a huge mountain chain of emotional peaks. But the two highest peaks in the play, Pelion and Ossa on Olympus, are the play-scene in which a crafty murder is enacted and the sword-play in the final scene when crafty murders and killings are committed. The two scenes are presented as public entertainments and they require more actors on stage at one time than most of the other scenes. In III. ii there are eleven speaking parts, and several mute attendants and lords would be used as members of a stage audience. In V. ii seven speakers are required and again we may suppose mute courtiers present to observe the sword-play.

These general correspondences are reinforced by the similarities in the complex structural designs of the two scenes. There is obviously the basic difference that the play-scene, occurring in the middle of the action, resolves one sequence of events and prepares us for the continuation of another, whereas the sword-play brings all action to a conclusion. There is a coda of a hundred lines after the play-within-the-play (III. ii. 284–384) preparing for Hamlet's meeting with Gertrude, in which the Prince mocks Rosencrantz and Guildenstern about the recorders and Polonius about the shape of the clouds. For the purposes of structural comparison I will leave out this sequence which links the action forward.

In separating out the major movements of the action and the build-up of the segments of interaction we can observe how much the rhythms of these two 'entertainments' have in common. Each scene divides into four distinct phases. The method of anticipation, building suspense, reaching the climactic trap, and then unfolding the consequences of the trap is the same in each case.

Act III, Scene ii (1–284)

A. Anticipation of the entertainment (1–86)

(i)   Hamlet advises the players about maintaining decorum in their acting. Though the discussion is general the concern with the skill which the entertainment requires is relevant to the performance of 'The Mousetrap' at the climax of the scene. 1–43.

(ii)   Polonius, Rosencrantz and Guildenstern arrive to announce that an audience is ready to gather for the play. 44–9.

(iii)   Hamlet praises Horatio and the audience discovers that he has enlisted his friend's aid in observing whether Claudius will betray his guilt at the play. 50–86.

B. Prologue to the entertainment (87–129)

(i)   The audience gathers and Hamlet exchanges pleasantries with Claudius, Polonius and Gertrude. 87–104.

(ii)   Hamlet seems to make an effort at reconciliation with Ophelia. 105–29.

C. The entertainment as trap (130–260)

(i)   The dumb-show, because it threatens to reveal the trap, heightens the suspense. 130.

(ii)   The first pause in the entertainment is devoted to an exchange between Hamlet and Ophelia. 130–45.

(iii)   The performance of the players continues. 146–220.

(iv)   The second pause shows Hamlet exchanging comments with the Queen, Claudius, and Ophelia. 221–44.

(v)   'The Mousetrap' reaches its climax. 245–50.

(vi)   The King reacts to the springing of the trap with a hasty departure. 251–60.

D. A commentary on the results of the entertainment as trap (261–84)

Horatio endeavours to calm down the exuberant Hamlet and they confirm agreement on Claudius' guilt. 261–84.

We find a similar general unfolding of events, with some significant variations, in the final scene.

Act V, Scene ii (1–392)

A. Anticipation of the entertainment (1–213)

(i)   Hamlet explains to Horatio how he escaped Claudius's plan for his death in England. This celebration of survival has an ironical ring because of the audience's knowledge of Claudius's latest secret stratagem to which Hamlet is about to fall innocent victim. 1–80.

(ii)   Osric arrives to broach Claudius's wager on a proposed encounter in sword-play of Laertes with Hamlet. The skills required in the 'entertainment' are discussed. 81–185.

(iii)   A Lord announces that the audience is ready to gather for the sword-play. 186–97.

(iv)   Hamlet indicates to Horatio that he has misgivings about the match but is determined to proceed. 198–213.

B. Prologue to the entertainment (214–68)

(i)   Hamlet generously reconciles himself with Laertes. 214–47.

(ii)   Foils are chosen and Claudius indicates how a victory by Hamlet will be celebrated. 248–68.

C. The entertainment as trap (269–347)

(i)   Suspense is heightened by the initial passes in sword-play which have no dire consequences. The first pass. 269–70.

(ii)   At the first pause there is a flourish of trumpets and the firing of cannons. The King invites Hamlet to drink but the stoup of poisoned wine is set aside. 270–3.

(iii)   The second bout of sword-play is also won by Hamlet. 274–5.

(iv)   In the second pause the Queen drinks to Hamlet's health and Laertes decides, though almost against his conscience, to spring his trap. 276–89.

(v)   The sword-play reaches its climax as the Queen dies of poison. Laertes, mortally wounded by his own treachery, reveals the three-pronged plot in which Hamlet has been fatally caught. Hamlet kills Claudius. 290–320.

(vi)   Hamlet, ensnared in the trap, bids farewell to Horatio, begs him to report his cause aright, and dies. 321–47.

D. A commentary on the results of the entertainment as trap (348–92)

Horatio, the lone remaining figure who can explain the slaughter, promises to Fortinbras and the court an account of all the causes of the fatal action. Fortinbras gives instructions for the preparation of Hamlet's funeral. 348–92.

There are many general structural parallels and several correspondences in specific detail between the two scenes. The relative weighting of
the different phases of the action varies considerably. It takes only 130
lines in III. ii before we get to the central action of the entertainment as
trap. Because of the verbal duelling with Osric it takes twice as long to get
to the sword-play in the final scene. The nature of the entertainment
varies also. In the play we have the spoken script as a lengthy accompani-
ment to the re-enactment of Claudius's crime. In the sword-play we have
a good deal of physical action with relatively few lines of script. The
process, however, of catching an enemy unawares is very much the same.

The initial phase in each scene is developed to exhibit to us Hamlet at
his wittiest and most gracious. We see more clearly than at any other
moment in the play the truth of Fortinbras's eventual eulogy that 'he was
likely, had he been put on. To have proved most royal' (V. ii. 386–7).
There is emphasis in each scene on the strength of the Prince's friendship
with Horatio, the only man he can trust. Their touching moments of
friendly appreciation and concern for each other (III. ii. 50–86; V. ii.
198–213) only highlight the loneliness and singular responsibility the
Prince must endure in his dangerous task. In each of the scenes we see
Hamlet interacting with one of Polonius's children and he seems to be
trying to resolve or put to rest the bitterness or confusion that they feel as
a result of his past actions. We feel that in each case he is trying, quite
mistakenly, to exempt himself from any further instrumentality in their
lives. In both of the scenes Hamlet has passing exchanges in the midst of
the performance with his mother. In the play-scene his barbs prepare us
for his outbreak of fury in the bedroom scene. In the sword-play
Gertrude's solicitude for her son seems to be an attempt to reassert her
position as a caring mother which he had so bitterly disputed in the
bedroom scene.

The secret murder buried in the past, Hamlet's assumption of an antic
disposition, and Claudius's murderous plots ensure that in all the scenes
of the play most of the characters are ignorant of what is really going on
and of the purposes for which they are being exploited by the protagonists. It is in these two scenes that the prevalent style of action in the play is
most clearly exhibited. In a later analysis I will explore in detail the play's
method of indirection. The two key scenes are the most crowded and the
most formal scenes in the play and the tension arises from our awareness
that there is much more going on than meets the eyes of most of the
audience on stage. Both scenes are traps, plays-within-plays. In both
scenes there are nervous interruptions from the setter of the trap urgent
in his concern that his quarry should not escape. As the stage-audience

innocently enjoys the sport we watch the victim move closer to the springing of the trap. In III. ii we are with Hamlet and Horatio, alertly observing whether the Ghost's testimony can be confirmed by giveaway reactions from the King. The play requires a slight adjustment to achieve its effect – the dozen or sixteen lines interpolated by Hamlet. The sword-play comes to us as two events; for everyone save Claudius, Laertes, and possibly Osric who shuffles the foils, it is mere entertaining exercise for a wager. To catch his unsuspecting nephew Claudius has made a number of adjustments – the unbated, envenomed foil and the poisoned cup. Public events are used for private ends beyond the comprehension of virtually all the courtiers present. In the first entertainment everyone survives, but a ghost's testimony is confirmed. In the second entertainment only Horatio, of the major characters, survives in the accomplishment of a ghost's demand for revenge. Both scenes, in a sense, show us an engineer hoist with his own petard. Hamlet discovers what he needs to know but in doing so reveals the sham of his antic disposition and provides Claudius with an excuse to ship him to England. The revenge he seeks must be postponed and becomes almost intractably difficult because his antagonist now has every reason to kill him first. Claudius's trap works only too well. He who had to watch in horror the enactment of the poisoning of his brother watches helplessly the poisoning of the wife he had won in that treachery and must himself drain off the poison and be stabbed by the envenomed foil he had intended for his nephew.

No audience will register all of the correspondences of detail. A director aware of the structural similarities will, however, produce a rhythm to the action which allows the audience to recognize that Shakespeare has made a deliberate link between the trap which Hamlet sets to surprise Claudius and the trap which, as a consequence, Claudius eventually sets to surprise Hamlet. An indispensable cue which highlights the connection is the placing of the King and Queen on their seats in the same position for both entertainments, the positioning of Horatio as an observer and the general grouping of attendant courtiers in the same positions on each occasion. If the sword-play occupies the same stage space as that formerly employed by the players of 'The Murder of Gonzago' then the rich implications of metadrama unfold the larger pattern of the play. The play gets its momentum from the Ghost's account of how he was caught unawares and murdered in his sleep. In the pivotal scene of the action strolling players, in all innocence, re-enact that murder and catch Claudius unawares. Hamlet is given one opportunity to take his revenge. He cannot bring himself to use the behind-the-back treachery of killing Claudius at his prayers, unprotected and with his guard down. Old Hamlet had been killed in his orchard while at rest. All the action which stems from that crime concludes with the killing of his son while he is 'at play'. The scenes I have examined contain very many structural similarities and yet lead to totally different consequences which are related to the temperaments of the two men who organize the entertainments. The Prince's plot is successful but it involves only the imitation of the action of murder. The only insurance Hamlet uses are Horatio's eyes to confirm his own observations. Claudius in the play-scene, is, as Hamlet asserts, 'frighted with false fire', the flash of powder from a blank discharge in a cannon which contains no shot. Claudius's entertainment is, despite surface appearances, conducted not with blanks, with false fire, but with unbated, envenomed foils and a poisoned cup as further insurance. Cannons, presumably firing blanks, are set off to signal Hamlet's initial success in the sword-play. But at the end they must be fired again, on Fortinbras's orders, to honour Hamlet in death. The 'false fire' is not now the death of a player-king but the homage due to a man who will never play the role of king.

2 · 'Thrice three times the value of this bond'

The three trials in *The Merchant of Venice*

In all of his plays Shakespeare presents us with a great variety of scenic structures, alternating soliloquy and intimate two- and three-character interactions with occasional large-scale scenes, which are often formal or public events, containing up to eight or nine speaking parts and the presence of several mute attendants. The Elizabethan playwrights were well advised, given the bareness of the stage in the public theatres and the limited possibilities of achieving any complex variety of stage effects, not to demand concentration on any one scene for an extended period. The scenic mosaic of the multiple plot, the rapid switch from courtiers to servants, from one locale to another, from sublime poetry to bawdy jests in prose indicates the commitment the writers had to variety. Yet one of the inherent dangers of the loosely structured, episodic plot is that in a long string of brief scenes a play may dissipate its energy and fail to produce the climactic tension and release which an audience demands. Many of the plays of this period, to use a food analogy, are like an extended series of snacks and appetizers without any meaty main course. Audiences have an appetite for full-scale dramatic confrontation – something that they and the actors can get their teeth into. Every Shakespeare play has a series of main courses, key scenes which present the emotional high points of the action. The audience feels a deep satisfaction at the end of them, in any production which can transmit the rhythm of the play, because a full involvement in such complex turning points is the best that drama can offer us. No audience is capable of cramming down one main course after another so the dramatic fare is varied. Nor is there any rule which dictates that a climactic turning point must occur in a long and complex scene. Some of the greatest scenes in Shakespeare are the more effective because of their brevity as we can see in the reuniting of Lear and Cordelia in the spare ninety-seven lines of IV. vii in *King Lear* or the murder of Duncan in the seventy-three lines of

II. ii in *Macbeth*. Nor do Shakespeare's most complex scenes have to be divided up between many characters. Five characters take part in III. iii in *Othello*, one of the most breathtaking scenes that Shakespeare ever wrote, but for almost three-quarters of the 480 lines we watch Iago working alone on the Moor, turning him, in one continuous sweep of stage action, from a noble and trusting husband into a tormented, murderous avenger. It is however, often true that the master scenes around which the rhythmic rise and fall of the action is organized are lengthy and complex sequences of events in which many characters take a share. Few of Shakespeare's plays contain more than a handful of scenes that are over 300 lines long. After we have chopped from plot to plot and place to place in short scenes the longer scenes often acquire a certain dramatic weight in their formal complexity. They often involve ceremony, the dignity and authority of public occasions, or the violation of ceremonial order. In the history plays Shakespeare developed many formal council scenes as occasions of violent, political confrontation. The deposition scene in *Richard II* is one of the pinnacles of his achievement in scenic structures. The Venetian senate in *Othello*, the scene at the Capitol where Caesar is murdered, the banquet scene in *Macbeth*, the play scene in *Hamlet*, the council scene at the opening of *King Lear* are all public occasions where a large number of the dramatis personae can be plausibly brought on stage together to produce a climactic event. In a theatre which used a good deal of 'doubling' the scenes which required that all of the available actors be on stage at once would, of necessity, have to be spaced out and surrounded by shorter scenes limited to fewer characters. The rhythms of a play are considerably influenced by these practical matters, most obviously in the way that final scenes can usually involve many characters because the actors, in one or other of their roles, no longer involved in costume changes, are all available. On the enormous bare, thrust stage of the public theatres a scene gains weight simply by the numbers of characters involved, by the orchestration of their entrances and exits, and by the groupings and movements which can be organized to point the action. The Elizabethan stage with its great depth and its two principal entrances in the tiring house wall, was not, in any case, suitable for any extended series of scenes which involved mass entrances and exits. Shakespeare constantly exercised his ingenuity in phasing a series of entrance and exits in the long scenes which involve many speakers. It was a technique that he was able to adapt to the rapid cut and thrust of battle action built up in a mosaic of incidents. We have only fully rediscovered the rhythms of Shakespeare's plays by performing them once again on flexible thrust stages. The long scenes with many characters interacting are often the culmination of events developed in a sequence of shorter scenes and they are usually placed at widely separated intervals in the play. We can often tell a good deal about the structure of a play if we can see how the master scenes are related to each other.

I have seen many productions of *The Merchant of Venice* but I have never attended one that I considered completely successful. The difficulties in staging it have, I think, as much to do with its structure as with modern reactions to the treatment of Shylock. The first half of the play strings together a series of episodic actions without focusing our attention in any long scenes. There is a deal of scaffolding erected before any major platform is laid down on which the major characters can engage in extended interaction. The longest scene in the first half of the play is II. ii and at 192 lines it seems of excessive length for the mere side issue of the Launcelot Gobbo clown routines it contains. The drift of the action is towards the resolution of the suit of Bassanio to Portia, and of the bond between Shylock and Antonio. All three of the play's major scenes, the climactic casket scene (III. ii), the trial scene (IV. i), and the resolution of the story in Belmont (V. i) are crowded into the second half of the play. A rough division of the play gives us 1253 lines in thirteen scenes until the casket scene, and then 1310 lines in seven scenes, of which the three major scenes occupy 1088 lines. It is unusual for Shakespeare to delay for so long the presentation of a complex, extended scene in which the action developed at the outset is brought to some sort of momentary climax which provides also a kind of springboard for the remaining action. Nor is it his habitual method to stack up long scenes involving many characters in such a close sequence. In the twenty scenes of the play ten have three or fewer speaking parts, five scenes have five speaking parts but in four of those one of the parts is a messenger or servant present only briefly. There are only the three major scenes which contain more than 200 lines. The last of the casket scenes (III. ii) has 326 lines and has seven speaking parts. There are also several mute bystanders in the trains of Bassanio and Portia. The trial scene (IV. i) is 455 lines long and has seven speaking parts and several mute attendants. The final ring scene in Belmont (V. i) is 307 lines long, has nine speakers as well as musicians and followers dressing the stage.

The play is unusual in what one might describe as 'the slow burn' of its structure, but it is organized on a deliberate principle which stems from the triadic sequence of trials which occur in the folk-tale sources. Much of the habit of developing scenic structures to repeat and vary the action is inherited from the romances and folk tales which furnish a large proportion of the sources for Elizabethan plays, as well as from the cyclic pattern of events laid down in the chronicle sources of the history plays. Those who were raised, and who raise their children, listening to fairy tales are never likely to forget the key significance of the formulaic structure of events: the three brothers (oldest, second, youngest) who undergo three separate quests and who confront witches, giants, dragons, etc. in three separate trials, often on successive days. The reward also is usually threefold – the bride, the kingdom, happiness ever after. What we celebrate and enjoy so often in Shakespeare is variety, the way he avoids rigidly repetitive patterns by allowing the plays to grow organically out of the individual needs of plot and character. The habit of using a variety of building blocks, alternating plots, short scenes, long scenes, etc. is always there in the most general sense but is never used with any formulaic inflexibility. In the various sources of *The Merchant of Venice* we find three trials, the love test, the entrapment and trial of a merchant, and the test of the rings. In *Il Pecorone* Gianetto only wins his lady on his third voyage. Shakespeare took the various elements of his play from different sources and found in the triple love test of *Il Pecorone* a structure which could be used in all the major events of his plot. The play weaves three strands of action together, the winning of Portia by Bassanio, the resolution of Shylock's bond with Antonio, the relationship developed between Jessica and Lorenzo. The bond itself is based on a borrowing of 3000 ducats for three months. In the drawing up of the bond (I. iii) the amount is stated seven times and the term six times, and there are other passing references to the number three in the same scene (67–70, 153–5).

In examining the three major scenes in the play we can see how a structural pattern, in a basic method of triadic development, is repeated though the action, tone and mood of the scenes vary considerably. The fundamental pattern of the trial of the caskets is laid down in the scene with Morocco II.vii) and with Arragon (II. ix). The action of each occasion is in three phases: (i) the consideration of the varying messages on the caskets; (ii) the climactic choice of one of the caskets; (iii) the consideration of the message within and the reactions of the suitor and of Portia. The relative foolishness of the first suitors and their choices of gold and silver give us assurance that Bassanio will be successful. Though it may seem to be something of a foregone conclusion Shakespeare devotes a good deal of space to the final casket scene. The audience has been waiting for this moment, this resolution of the action in a major ceremonial occasion, for twelve scenes and it needs the release. The play's mosaic of scenes moves us from one plot to the other and variety is provided along the way with the clowning of Launcelot and Old Gobbo and the elopement of Lorenzo and Jessica. In the major scenes which provide a culmination to a sequence of action Shakespeare usually avoids any blurring of impact or dissipation of energy by eliminating marginal matters. He creates a sweeping crescendo of tension focused on one particular dramatic issue. Such scenes often achieve even greater clarity by organizing themselves around something physically specific. In the major scenes of *The Merchant of Venice* we have the caskets, the pound of flesh nearest Antonio's heart, and the rings which Portia and Nerissa have inveigled out of their husbands.

Bassanio's trial of the caskets repeats the firmly established pattern of a ceremonial ritual in the consideration of the three riddling messages. The action unfolds in an unhurried manner and Portia's song helps to increase the air of enchantment in Belmont. To this point only three scenes have exceeded half the length of this scene; eight of the thirteen scenes have 100 lines or less.

Act III, Scene ii

First phase (1–185)

(i)   Portia tries to persuade Bassanio to delay his choice but he insists on undergoing the trial. 1–62.

(ii)   Bassanio considers the casket and makes his choice. 63–107.

(iii)   He reads the message in the lead casket, reacts to it, and Portia joyously yields to him. 108–85.

Second phase (186–296)

(i)   Gratiano and Nerissa announce their marriage plans. 186–219.

(ii)   Lorenzo and Jessica arrive. Salerio brings news of Antonio's wounded fortunes. 220–96.

Third phase (297–326)

(i)   Portia sends Bassanio off to pay Antonio's debt twenty times over. 297–326.

In the six segments of the scene passages of seventy to eighty lines alternate with units of around thirty lines. The first phase of the scene is a repetition of the earlier casket scenes and the action thereafter introduces material which links us forward to the trial scene in Venice and to the mock trial of faith in the ring episode which concludes the story in the return to Belmont. The structural core of the scene is the embrace the triumphant Bassanio shares with Portia and her yielding up of her estate and her ring to him. It takes 148 lines to reach Portia's speech of generous yielding (149–74). When her speech concludes there are 152 lines remaining in the scene so its centrality is quite precisely emphasized. Portia's behaviour, in a threefold development, is the key to the scene's structure. She starts out eager to postpone the trial because she fears to lose Bassanio's company. In the middle she joyfully commits her life to him forever. At the end she gives an example of her generosity in hazarding all by urging Bassanio's instant departure to save his friend even though it means that she and Nerissa must start off married life as maids and widows. Bassanio wins a fortune and a new direction to his life in the person of Portia. In the midst of this gain comes news of the threat of total loss – Antonio's ruin and his expectation of death. It seems as if the new bond of love has enough generosity in it to cancel the bond of hate on which Shylock is framing his revenge. The scene also brings together for the first time in the play the triad of young lovers.

Shakespeare uses the structural design of his scenes to indicate a gradual change in Portia's position. In the most general terms of organization Shakespeare's scenic structures are of two types. The first type, and by far the commonest, is that in which one or more of the characters enter to be joined, in phases, by other characters who may depart separately or at the scene's end. Such scenes give us a sequence of shifts in focus in what can be described as episodic interaction. The second type brings on the characters together at the outset, has them develop the whole scene between them and exit more or less together. These are scenes of single-focus interaction. Of necessity, because they are not interrupted and attention is not redirected by a sequence of comings and goings, such scenes are often more static, less concerned with a complex intertwining of events. In *The Merchant of Venice* all but five of the twenty scenes have a structure of episodic interaction. It is significant that three of the five single-focus scenes involve Portia. In the four-and-a-half scenes in which she appears until Bassanio has triumphed in his trial of the caskets, she is interrupted briefly only twice by messengers with news of the arrival of suitors. Though suitors come and go the scenes, in their simple structure, give emphasis to our impression of Portia as a fly stuck in amber, trapped almost to the point of enchantment by the terms of the test which her father left in his will. The sense of seclusion in Belmont, with Portia a not-too-distant relative in folk-tale motifs of Sleeping Beauty, is emphasized in the language as well as in the scenic designs. Immediately following Bassanio's rescuing of Portia from the imprisoning terms of the casket test, Lorenzo and Jessica arrive in Belmont as refugees as though at last Portia's secluded life can be opened up to the flux of events in the outside world. Almost at once Portia moves out of Belmont to take a principal role in that hard world of commercial calculations. Every scene in which she appears for the rest of the play has an episodic structure and that helps to emphasize her flexibility, vitality and sharpness of wit which were given such little scope in the moated grange atmosphere of fairy-tale enchantment.

There are, after Bassanio's departure to save Antonio, only some 200 lines in three brief scenes before Shakespeare begins the climactic confrontation of the trial in Venice. Only the fooling of Launcelot and the love chat of Lorenzo and Jessica (III. v) are tangential to this trial. The casket scene, which demonstrates how life affirming it is to hazard everything for love and friendship, seals the bond of marriage. With very little pause we are confronted by Shylock's business bond which will forgive nothing and will prey on flesh itself. The trial scene is the central arch in the structure of the play and, at 455 lines, is by far the longest scene. It is the only scene in which Portia and Shylock, the representatives of the two juxtaposed forces of love and hate, meet. Portia has had to endure patiently the constricting terms of the bond of the casket. She finds a way to use the constricting terms of Shylock's business bond to tie him up.

The trial in Venice has a prologue before Shylock enters and an epilogue after his departure. In defining the various segments of the scene we can observe the careful balance which Shakespeare achieves in building up to a climax and then bringing us down from it. Almost exactly halfway through the scene (223) Portia asks Shylock for the bond and begins to turn the tide against him. Until that point Portia concerns herself with an appeal for mercy which supersedes the letter of the law. Falling symmetrically after this central point is her interpretation of the bond in the strictest legal terms. Symmetrically arranged before and after these arguments are, at the outset, the offer to Shylock of sums of money much larger than those nominated in the bond and, at the end, Shylock's pleading when he is trapped merely for the money owed to him and the court's refusal to yield even that to him. The triadic structures prominent in the play are especially prominent in this scene. Each of the three places of action in the scene divides into three parts.

Act IV, Scene i

Prologue. Before Shylock enters the Duke pities Antonio because of the merciless nature of the man pursuing him. 1–15.

First phase (16–118)

1st appeal (i) The Duke indicates that he expects mercy from Shylock. 16–34.

          (ii) Shylock indicates that he will have 'the due and forfeit of my bond'. 35–62.

2nd appeal (i) Bassanio appeals for mercy and offers double the 3000 ducats nominated in the bond. 63–84.

          (ii) Shylock rejects the offer. 85–7.

3rd appeal (i) The Duke asks Shylock how he can hope for mercy when he renders none. 88.

          (ii) Shylock in reply demands his pound of flesh. 89–103.

Interlude. The Duke refers to Bellario's judgment. Gratiano reviles Shylock while the court awaits the arrival of Bellario's 'young doctor'. 104–63.

Second phase (164–344)

1st appeal (i) After a few cursory questions Portia restates the Duke's initial plea for mercy. 164–203.

          (ii) Shylock rejects it. 204–5.

2nd appeal (i) Portia draws from Bassanio a repetition of his offer to repay the money, threefold or tenfold if necessary. Shylock rejects all offers and prepares to carve Antonio's flesh. 206–60.

          (ii) Antonio prepares for death and bids farewell to his friends. 261–302.

3rd appeal Portia turns the tables on Shylock by allowing him the terms of his bond, but she reminds him that he must adhere to its smallest scruple. 303–44. There are three stages in Shylock's climbing down from his demands in hope of salvaging something from the wreckage.

          (i) Shylock accepts the original offer of thrice the bond. Bassanio is willing to give it but Portia insists that he take the flesh instead. 316–33.

(ii) Shylock asks only for his principal back. Despite Bassanio's willingness to give up the sum Portia refuses the amount. 334–42.

(iii) Shylock abandons hope of any return on the bond and declares he will leave. 343–44.

Third phase (345–98)

Shylock resisted three appeals twice and yielded in three steps any hope of payment. He is now subjected to a three-pronged attack of imposed penalties.

1st penalty. Portia asserts that half of Shylock's goods are forfeit to Antonio and half to the state. 345–52.

2nd penalty. She declares that Shylock's very life lies in the mercy of the Duke. 353–70.

3rd penalty. Antonio gives his judgment on his enemy in three conditions. 378–88.

    (i) Shylock must leave his goods in trust for Lorenzo and Jessica.

    (ii) Shylock must convert to Christianity.

    (iii) Shylock must record a gift of all he dies possessed of to Lorenzo and Jessica.

Epilogue. After Shylock's departure Portia, with the excuse of urgent business, refuses the Duke's invitation to dinner. 399–405.

Shakespeare elaborated this complex structure out of the much simpler details in *Il Pecorone*. There we find that various multiples of the debt have been offered to the merchant before the trial scene and have been rejected. There is in the trial no phased series of appeals for mercy building up to the climactic moment when the trap is sprung. Gianetto's lady in her disguise as a lawyer makes, on her entrance, an immediate challenge to the merchant to take the flesh but no blood. Nor are the penalties in *Il Pecorone* as elaborate as Shakespeare makes them. The merchant bargains for lesser amounts, but when he is denied he tears up his bond and departs. There is no forfeiting of wealth to the state, to the man he would have killed, nor any stipulation of a conversion to Christianity.

The last segment of this scene (406–55) is a bridge passage which prepares the ground for the action in the rest of the play. It falls into three sections.

(i)   Bassanio and Antonio offer thanks and Portia considers herself
       well paid. 406–18.
(ii)   Bassanio insists that she take a token of their gratitude. Portia
       asks for gloves and a ring. When Bassanio refuses her she
       departs. 419–46.
(iii) Antonio begs Bassanio to satisfy her request and so Gratiano is
       sent off with the ring. 447–55.

Thus Shakespeare changes the mood at the end of the trial scene away
from severity and retribution towards the comic mock-trial of love with
which the play concludes. This coda about the ring is, in fact, a
light-hearted variation on what has been a central preoccupation in the
trial. Antonio, threatened with the loss of something infinitely valuable,
his life, has various supporters who ask Shylock to accept very much
more money than the bond demands. When Portia asks Bassanio for a
mere trifle, the ring, she demands that which is dearest to him. He offers
her any other ring of infinitely greater value as a substitute. Antonio did
not have to yield up his life nor did Shylock get the substitute he was
offered. Portia wants only what she asks for and she gets it. In one trial
Antonio, in keeping faith in the bond contracted on his friend's behalf,
comes perilously close to losing a pound of flesh next to his heart. In the
other trial Bassanio, in comic desperation in trying to conceal the breach
he believes he has made in his bond of love with Portia, considers it were
best to cut his left hand off and swear that he lost the ring defending it (V.
i. 177–8).

The ring scene at Belmont is, then, a test of faith but, in comparison to
the two earlier tests, it is a mock-trial in a holiday mood. Shakespeare
approaches this test in a gentle, lyrical love scene. The scene is organized
in three phases which present us first with harmony, then with wrangling
and finally with a renewal of harmony. There are eighty-eight lines
before Portia enters, 126 lines before Bassanio enters and almost half of
the scene is over before there is any mention of the rings. The opening
sequence is, however, in its mood and in its concern with harmony, very
pertinent to the trial which ensues.

Act V, Scene i

First phase.

A harmonious mood at Belmont is established and the trial of the two
husbands is set up (1–126)

(i)   Lorenzo and Jessica, in something close to a song in two-part harmony, give testimony of their love. 1–24.

(ii)   A messenger arrives announcing Portia's arrival. 25–38. Launcelot indicates that Bassanio's arrival is imminent. 39–48.

(iii)   Lorenzo speaks to Jessica of the nature of harmony in music, in planetary motions and in animals. 49–88.

(iv)   Portia and Nerissa arrive. They swear Lorenzo and Jessica to silence about their absence. 89–126.

Second phase.

The ring test of Bassanio and Gratiano (127–253)

(i)   Welcome is given to Bassanio and Antonio. 127–41.

(ii)   Both Nerissa and Portia challenge their husbands about the rings they have given away. 142–222.

(iii)   Portia indicates that in order to punish their husbands for their betrayal the wives must be as liberal and as unconcerned about true faith. 223–53.

Third phase.

The revelation of the truth about the rings and news of sudden good fortune (254–307)

(i)   The revelation of the identity of the lawyer and the clerk show that the ring trial has been a jest. 254–73.

(ii)   Antonio receives news about his recovered argosies. 273–88.

(iii)   The news for Lorenzo and Jessica of the wealth they will inherit is followed by the conclusion of the play. 289–307.

The whole play in its culmination in three major scenes has a symmetry around the trial in Venice. The two love scenes in Belmont are arranged one before and one after the settlement of mercenary issues in the courtroom. In order to get from the initial joy in Bassanio's triumph at the caskets to the witty love scene at the conclusion Portia has to escape for a while the refined atmosphere of Belmont. In archetypal terms she takes something akin to a journey to the underworld when she confronts in Venice a brutal, grasping, inhuman desire to capitalize on a forfeited bond. She confronts the cannibal monster, Shylock, defeats him and emerges unscathed and unrecognized. If a production cannot communicate a sense of the relatedness of the three major scenes of this play then it usually fails. Many critics have found the final scene lightweight, an anomalous coda not quite convincingly tied in with the rest of the play. As the final element in the three-part rhythm the light practical joke helps to dispel the enchanted castle atmosphere that has lingered over Belmont. Lorenzo and Jessica submit to the magic spell of the place. Shakespeare indicates in a broader, humanizing action that it will have to accommodate the give and take of married life. There is a gradual movement in the play away from the ceremonial rhetoric in the somewhat sinister test of the caskets first to the sharp and bitter ironies of the courtroom and then to the private and racier language of domestic teasing. Jests about betrayed wives and cuckolded husbands are the stuff of a good deal of comedy. The young lovers in their struggle with Shylock have had a strangely postponed introduction to marriage. The joke which the women play is not original, nor even very funny, but it moves us towards a world of normality far from the hideous unnaturalness of Shylock sharpening his knife to carve his pound of flesh. It serves also as a vivid contrast to the static, hermetic world of the casket trials in which we first found Portia trapped.

The bonds in each of the three trials are linked together by the threat of penalties. When Bassanio confronts the caskets he risks, should he fail, not only all future contact with Portia but any chance of marriage as a normal expectation of his life. This is a detail added by Shakespeare for the source makes no mention of a penalty for failure in the trial. In hazarding all to gain all and in choosing the correct casket Bassanio avoids the penalty clause which would debar him from wooing any other maid. Antonio has hazarded all he has to give Bassanio his chance. Portia finds a way of making the bond which would take Antonio's life, penalize Shylock and divest him of all the wealth he has. Bassanio is given a ring as a bond of love. When he is confronted by his wife in a trial of his faith he is as incapable of meeting her demands as Antonio was of meeting Shylock's. Portia indicates that there is here also a penalty for forfeiture of the bond. She threatens to act as freely in distributing her favours as Bassanio has in giving away her ring. Bassanio, the young adventurer, with Antonio's help, came to Belmont to release Portia from the thralldom of the casket test. He finds that he has won not only a fortune, but also a witty and ingenious wife who can release Antonio from the threat of a tragic death, and who can win a test of faith more riddling and less amenable to solution than the test which had first brought them together. The casket test could be won only by someone who could see beyond superficial appearances. Shylock's bond can be defused only by seeing in it more than appears in its stated terms. The ring test could have been survived only by someone who could see through Balthazar's disguise.

The romance mode of the trial in Belmont gives place to the melodrama of the trial in Venice which in turn gives place to comedy, bordering on farce, in the trial of rings in the return to Belmont. Shakespeare found a way of linking the diverse moods of these scenes together by rhythmic repetitions in the structural designs of the trials.

3 · The journey from 'wherefore art thou Romeo?' to 'Where is my Romeo?'

The structure of *Romeo and Juliet*

Arthur Brooke's poem, *The Tragicall Historye of Romeus and Juliet*, begins with references to the two feuding households and with the Prince's efforts to control them, but it moves quickly to the plight of the lovelorn Romeus. Though Shakespeare took many details, with some significant modifications, from Brooke, the method of opening the story with a vivid street brawl involving servants, introducing Tybalt and Benvolio, and bringing on the parents and the Prince to crowd the stage, is entirely his own invention. Shakespeare establishes the feud not only for its arresting opening action but also as the structural framework around which all the details of the plot can be deployed. The whole play is developed in terms of remarkable symmetry around three scenes of tumultuously crowded action devoted to the feud, to sword-play and its consequences. After the initial feud scene we are concerned, in the first half of the play, with the development of the love of Romeo and Juliet and its culmination in their secret marriage. Following hard upon that happy occasion comes the turning point of the play where the feud, in its second outbreak, embroils Romeo (III. i. 129). The action then moves into desperate attempts to salvage the secret marriage which lead ineluctably to the third scene of brawling sword-play and death. The three scenes of violence contain similar component elements, but as the scenic pattern is repeated it is also extended to lead to ever more tragic consequences.

Many critics of the play have found its structure flawed in the way in which, in its first half, it seems to develop like a comedy, and then, in the second half, hustles towards tragedy by the stringing together of improbable accidents and coincidences. If we focus on the overarching structure which regulates the play, the three violent interventions of the feud, we can see how a series of parallel and contrasted scenes are related to them. In both halves of the play two actions run counter to each other. The Capulets, intent on bringing Juliet and Paris together, give a feast which allows Romeo to meet Juliet and their love draws in Friar Laurence to arrange a secret marriage. In the second half the Capulets hastily arrange a feast to celebrate the precipitate marriage of Paris to Juliet thus drawing Friar Laurence into desperate shifts to ensure the secret reuniting of Romeo and Juliet. In the confusion of cross purposes Romeo and Juliet are forced underground both figuratively and literally. It is the more or less normal surface flow of domestic events which highlights for us the desperate changes in circumstances for the young lovers. I will examine first the repetitions and changes in the scenic design of the three feud scenes. I will then examine the way in which the kinds of actions which occur between the opening scene and the turning point are echoed and altered in significance in the actions between the turning point and the final tragic outburst of violence.

The opening scene divides into two almost equal halves. The first part is devoted to the public issue of the feud as it breaks out in street brawling (1–113). In Brooke there is only a description of antagonistic families and no immediately vivid display of the feud in operation. The second half is concerned with the private family issue of Romeo's melancholy (114–236). The scene carefully juxtaposes the public issue of a stage crowded with Capulets and Montagues involved in verbal and physical abuse, a summer storm of rancorous confusion, with the private humours of an individual Montague and a leisurely discussion between Romeo and Benvolio, in ornate rhetorical figures, about the trials of unrequited love. Love and hate are forces which become tragically entangled in the play, but at the outset they are presented as oil and water still unmixed. Romeo, mooning in meadows, may be embroiled in love, and he is brought on only after the street brawl has died down. The feud is to him merely an excuse for elaborating poetical conceits on his own love-struck condition.

Act I, Scene i

Part 1. The public troubles of the feud

(i)   Two Capulet servants, Gregory and Sampson, discuss the feud. 1–31.

(ii) Two Montague servants, Abram and Balthazar, meet them and insults lead to brawling. 32–54.

(iii) A Montague, Benvolio, enters to stop the brawl. 55–62.

(iv)   A Capulet, Tybalt, enters to promote the feud. 63–9.

(v)   Citizens and officers enter the mêlée. 70–2.

(vi)   Old Capulet and his wife enter. 73–6.

(vii)   Montague and his wife enter. 77–8.

(viii)   The Prince quells the brawling of his rebellious subjects. 79–101.

(ix)   Montague and his wife, left alone with Benvolio, seek an explanation of the fighting. 102–13.

Part 2. The private troubles of Romeo

(i)   The Montagues try to elicit from Benvolio explanations for Romeo's melancholy behaviour. 114–57.

(ii)   Benvolio questions Romeo about his lovesick mood and Romeo, in the conventional terms of the courtly love code, elaborates on his relationship to his unattainable mistress. 158–236.

In this first outbreak of violence there are no deaths, but we learn from the Prince that this is one of a series of brawls which have 'thrice disturbed the quiet of our streets' (89). Many of the elements that will appear in the later scenes of sword-play are established here. We have Benvolio trying unsuccessfully to prevent fighting. There is the hothead Tybalt hungry for blood. The citizenry are aroused, the parents enter and argue. The Prince enters in time here to prevent bloodshed but he has to threaten death in the hope of instilling civil order. Benvolio has to report on the genesis of the fracas. In this scene there are fourteen character speakers and a few mute supers among the aroused citizens and the Prince's train. As in the later scenes we start with two speakers and then a whirlpool of violence draws more and more characters into the vortex of danger. Romeo, most conspicuously, avoids that vortex. The only important characters who have not appeared by the end of the first scene are Juliet, Mercutio, Paris, the Nurse and Friar Laurence. All but Friar Laurence are brought into the action in the subsequent three scenes. These (I. ii; I. iii; I. iv) build up the action in preparation for the only scene in the play where a crowd of characters on stage does not take part in, or arrive as witnesses to, the violent effects of sword-play (I. v).

Shakespeare with great care, in the crowded scene of the masked ball, leaves the Montagues and Capulets apart save for the first decisive contact between Romeo and Juliet. None of the masked visitors, except Romeo, has any verbal exchange with a Capulet. Mercutio has no lines and Benvolio has only one when he encourages Romeo to depart. The feast has eleven speakers and is tellingly structured in the way that it juxtaposes the hatred of one Capulet child, Tybalt, itching to fight Romeo, and the love of another, Juliet, eager to embrace him. The presence of the fiery Tybalt at the masked ball is Shakespeare's invention. In Brooke Tybalt makes his first appearance at the point where he fights and is killed by Romeus. Shakespeare's Tybalt, despite his fury, is prevented from saying anything directly to Romeo or any of his companions. Romeo exchanges words only with Juliet and the Nurse. The sparring between the families is maintained with great delicacy in the witty bargaining about hands, lips and prayers between the young lovers. But even though Capulet averts the threat of brawling we are made aware of the inescapable snares of the feud which will eventually trap Romeo. Until that explosion of the feud the action is devoted entirely to the development of the harmonious force of love. It involves witty mockery of Romeo, a variety of advice to him, go-betweens, and the secret arrangements for marriage. Only once in this sequence (II. iv) are there ever as many as five speakers on stage at one time. The action proceeds, unclouded by serious threats, until we reach the second summer storm in the central intercession of the feud.

Act III, Scene i

Part 1

(i)   As they idle in the streets Mercutio and Benvolio chaff each other about the touchy moods which lead them so quickly to pick a quarrel. 1–33.

(ii)   The fiery Tybalt enters and 'an airy word' provokes Mercutio. 34–54.

(iii)   When Romeo enters Tybalt tries, without success, to draw him into a fight. 55–71.

Part 2

(i)   Mercutio takes up the challenge and Romeo, trying to prevent the fight, is in part a cause of his friend's mortal injury. 72–88.

(ii)   The dying Mercutio curses both households. 89–106.

(iii)   Romeo recognizes a responsibility for Mercutio's injury. 107–13.

(iv)   Benvolio brings news to Romeo of Mercutio's death. 114–18.

(v)   On Tybalt's return Romeo feels compelled to enter the feud. He slays Tybalt and flees. 119–34.

(vi)   The citizens enter. 135–8.

Part 3

(i)   The Prince enters with the Capulets and the Montagues and receives a report from Benvolio of the fray. 139–84.

(ii)   The Prince passes a judgment of exile on Romeo. 184–95.

Romeo and Juliet contains 2993 lines in twenty-four scenes. There are eleven scenes before this pivotal scene and twelve scenes after it. Up to the moment when Romeo, by killing Tybalt (III. i. 129), becomes fortune's fool the play has run 1504 lines. There are 1489 lines remaining. The turning point is thus only a few lines from the precise mid-point. The symmetry is further underlined by the way the climax occurs in the middle sequence of a three-part scene. As long as Romeo resists, in this scene, the pressure to enter the feud the hopeful possibility that his match with Juliet will bring reconciliation to their families remains alive. From the moment Tybalt falls, no matter what desperate stratagems are devised, tragedy, by the deadly logic of the revenge code, is inevitable. The scene concludes with the first decision in a chain of consequences which lead to death's harvest in the final scene.

In this central scene, as in the opening action, verbal challenges lead quickly to sword-play. Once more Benvolio endeavours to defuse the situation. Once more Tybalt is the catalyst. Citizens, parents and the Prince are drawn into the vortex of violence. Again Benvolio must recount what has occurred. The Prince makes a second attempt to instil civil order by a stern judgment. But it is the alteration in the order of events and the additions that are more significant than the repetitions. This time the prologue to action is not among servants with their comic banter. It is a clash of major characters who cannot be held in check by Benvolio. In the earlier battle the parents were embroiled in the scuffling, but they enter now in time only to hear of their children's fates. The Prince had, at the outset, arrived before blood was shed, now he arrives only after death has plucked off two of his subjects. Romeo, who was off-stage in the first brawl, is now a principal actor in the feud. Mercutio, absent in the first scene, is killed in this one. All of the other characters are unchanged. Of the major characters only Paris, the Nurse, Juliet and Friar Laurence are absent. The most obvious continuing link is Prince Escalus for he appears on stage only in the three scenes of violence. His inability to enforce his will on this turbulent society is evident in the delays in his intervention. The death he promises offenders at the outset is commuted to banishment in Romeo's case. But the audience recognizes that it is merely a postponement of the inevitable. The progression from sword-play to the death of major characters, one of them not a blood relative of the feuding families, can only spread to engulf the principals.

Although the basic elements of this scene owe a good deal to Brooke the changes which Shakespeare introduced are quite significant. In Brooke a street brawl breaks out between the Montagues and the Capulets, who are led by Tybalt. Romeus enters to prevent strife, is drawn into battle by Tybalt, kills him, and flees. The roused Prince enters and passes the judgment of banishment on Romeus. Shakespeare transferred this general mêlée to his first scene. He starts out his central scene with the leisurely jesting of Mercutio and Benvolio, characters who have no originals in Brooke. Tybalt enters, not as he had in the first scene and in Brooke to urge on large-scale street fighting, but to provoke a private duel. The way Shakespeare draws Romeo into the feud through loyalty to Mercutio is a much more complex sequence of action than Brooke had presented. Nor is there, in Brooke, any reference to parents appealing for justice over the dead bodies, nor any figure like Benvolio reporting the battle.

After this public scene the play, in its second half, turns again to more domestic, private events. Until the final scene of violent, misadventured deaths no scene presents us with more than five speakers sharing the stage at one time. Seven of the eleven scenes are devoted to interactions between three characters or less.

When violence invades the stage for the last time it is not as an outbreak of the feud itself but as a consequence of the secrecy and plotting which the feud has enforced. From a calm opening we move quickly to sword-play and death and ultimately to a stage crowded with the survivors in a society despoiled of its youth.

Act V, Scene iii

Part 1

(i)   Paris, with his page, comes to strew flowers on Juliet's tomb. 1–21.

(ii)   Romeo, with Balthazar, comes to view the 'dead' Juliet. 22–48.

(iii) Paris interrupts Romeo and is killed in a sword fight. 49–73.

Part 2

(i)   Romeo, alone, laments his loss of Juliet and poisons himself. 74–120.

(ii)   Friar Laurence and Balthazar discover the dead Romeo. 121–47.

(iii) The Friar tells the awakening Juliet of the miscarried plans. 148–59.

(iv)   Juliet, left alone, says farewell to Romeo and stabs herself. 160–70.

Part 3

(i)   In sequence Paris's page, the watchmen, Balthazar and the Friar arrive. 171–87.

(ii)   The Prince and the Capulets enter. 188–207.

(iii) Montague arrives. 208–22.

(iv)   The Friar and Balthazar report on the events that have caused the deaths. The Prince asserts that all are punished. 223–95.

(v)   Montague is reconciled with the Capulets. 296–310.

The scene presents a variety of incidents, with interruptions, sudden violence and a stage filling with characters too late once again to prevent catastrophe. The elements are familiar, challenges, sword-play, failed attempts to head off death, Friar Laurence serving as ineffectively as Benvolio before him. Events require clarification by report and Friar Laurence here also succeeds Benvolio in his narrative role. Despite a familiar progression of events it is the novel elements in the scene which ensure a tragic conclusion.

The most obvious change is in the locale. From the brawl of the morning we move to a second street battle in the heat of day and end in the confusion of a dark graveyard. The Montagues and Capulets, impelled by hate, engage in battles which lead to death. Finally a Montague and a Capulet, impelled by love, kill themselves. Paris, an innocent bystander who has had no part in the feud, nevertheless dies. In the last of the sequence of scenes plagued by violence Juliet is on stage for the first time, yet ironically she does not come soon enough to consciousness to prevent Romeo's suicide. In the three scenes Romeo moves from non-involvement, to violent participation, to death. In the first scene Romeo and Juliet had never met and in the last scene the married pair share the stage but can never again meet alive. A grisly symmetry is completed. Romeo, who had earlier threatened to kill himself with his dagger, dies by taking an apothecary's potion beside Juliet's 'corpse'. Juliet, who had taken the Friar's potion so that she might meet her husband, is left to despatch herself with his dagger beside his corpse. Of the six young people involved in the feud and its consequences five are dead. Benvolio, the only significant survivor of the earlier feud scenes, makes no appearance at the end. Though doubling probably is the reason for his absence it serves also to underline the survival only of the old. Of the five characters who have entered late in the three scenes – the four parents and the Prince – only Lady Montague is absent at the end. The Prince has failed twice to establish an order which could prevent tragedy and so he is left with a 'glooming peace' as the parents finally bury their enmity with the bodies of their children.

The ironical development of events within each of the three related scenes becomes progressively more sinister. In I. i we are liable to be amused by the initial comic posturings of servants as they warily egg each other on to a quarrel. Yet out of this banter grows a brawl which ends with the Prince's threat of death to those who persist. We turn again to amusement at the extravagant claims of the tormented Romeo. In despair for Rosaline he declares that his response to rejection is: 'in that vow/Do I live dead that live to tell it now' (I. i. 221–2). The audience's foreknowledge of the story adds a premonitory irony to the assertion. Within the two hours' traffic of the stage he will die in earnest for a woman who, he is unaware, lives dead in her tomb. In III. i we start out with Mercutio chaffing the peace-loving Benvolio about being tetchy, quarrelsome, and liable to fight on the slightest pretext. Before the end of the scene Benvolio is explaining how Mercutio, who objected to one word 'consort', used by Tybalt to characterize his friendship with Romeo, has come to be 'worms' meat'. Most sinister of all the sudden contingencies is the development in V. iii. We start with Paris bringing flowers to honour Juliet's tomb. His appearance at the tomb is an addition by Shakespeare to Brooke's story. Without knowing it, of course, Paris has arrived too early. By the end of the scene there will indeed be a dead Juliet and a grave where flowers would be appropriate. But by that time Paris is dead himself. He dies because he tries to stop Romeo, whom he suspects to be motivated by the feud, from breaking in to the Capulet monument. Paris never knows that his killer is a rival in love already secretly married to Juliet. The scene, which opens with young men arriving too early in mourning for a woman who is not yet dead, ends with many people arriving too late to do anything other than mourn those who failed, by mere seconds, to reunite alive.

These increasingly ominous exclamation marks punctuate with public violence what is otherwise a story devoted to domestic, private and secret actions. What strikes us about the first half of the action the more it recedes into memory in the darkening circumstances of the second half is that it was, relatively speaking, relaxed, brimming with innocence, and invested with a sense of play. There was time for gossip, and for dancing, for lingering on balconies, for a fellowship of young men to ramble the streets cracking bawdy jokes, for the teasing of the Nurse. This is signalled at all levels in the space allowed for the elaboration of complex and witty poetic figures, of which perhaps the Queen Mab speech is the most obvious example. The gaudy riches of the imagination are used to ornament the progress towards a marriage which society would deem impossible but which, nevertheless, comes to pass. The poetic riches in the second half are often used to express the feverish anxiety of those seeking to avoid a marriage which society deems possible but which can never come to pass. The freedom and play which accompanies love's triumph over hate in the first half turns to constricted circumstances and the earnest, oppressive, and ultimately impossible task of evading death.

The great scope of Shakespeare's plays has a good deal to do with the radical compression of a lifetime of emotional experiences into a few hours, which forces on our awareness at our last view of the characters the recall of where we had initially met them. Romeo, who at the end is forcing open the rotten jaws of the womb of death to cram it with more food, is the young man we first saw returning from a melancholy ramble in the meadows to elaborate idle love conceits at his leisure. Juliet, who initially endures the Nurse's interminable chatter about her infant precocity in bravely putting up with a bump on the forehead, becomes the despairing wife stabbing herself in a charnel house. When we first meet Paris he is being invited to a feast to woo Juliet. He never enjoys a marriage feast and dies in an unexpected encounter at Juliet's tomb. The reflective Friar we first meet philosophizing at leisure on the herbs he is gathering becomes the inventor of a fantastic plot which leaves him stumbling too late among gravestones.

Shakespeare thrusts the impact of these changes on us by setting up scenic structures in each half of the play which have similar surface elements but which differ completely in their moods and consequences. Our minds are thrown back by a recognition of pattern only to appreciate more fully the contrasts which a few hours have wrought. These echoing scenes are not set up in the same order in each half of the play, nor is there any consistency in the vividness of recall associated with the corresponding scenes. At times a very deliberate contrast within a similar basic structure is in the forefront of the audience's mind. In other matters we have only a sense of faint but persistent echoes which help us to gauge how matters are sliding towards tragedy. In both halves of the play Shakespeare maintains elements of comic banter, details of domestic preparation, parental advice and demands, Friar Laurence's secret stratagems.

The opening of I. ii presents thirty-seven lines of an interview between Capulet and his prospective son-in-law, Paris. The urgency of Paris's suit is initially tempered by Capulet's caution:

> My child is yet a stranger in the world,
> She hath not seen the change of fourteen years;
> Let two more summers wither in their pride
> Ere we may think her ripe to be a bride.
>
> (I. ii. 8–11)

When Paris presses his case with 'Younger than she are happy mothers made' (12), Capulet resists 'And too soon marred are those so early made' (13). He suggests, however, that Paris should attend his 'old accustomed feast' that evening, a lavish affair with many in attendance. There is a leisurely approach here in which Juliet, as one among many maidens, might not be the one Paris will finally choose:

> Hear all, all see,
> And like her most whose merit most shall be;
> Which, on more view of many, mine, being one,
> May stand in number, though in reck'ning none.
>
> (I. ii. 30–3)

Before the end of this scene Benvolio will urge Romeo to attend the ball so that he might temper his fond idolatry of Rosaline by comparing her her with other beauties (84–9, 96–101).

The reprise of the first Capulet-Paris interview comes in the thirty-six lines of III. iv. Now it is Paris who, with due decorum in respect of the family's grief over Tybalt's death, proposes delay: 'These times of woe afford no times to woo./Madam, good night. Commend me to your daughter' (8–9). Capulet, erratic, choleric and concerned to distract Juliet from the dangerous grief he presumes to be caused by her cousin's death, takes a surprisingly different attitude from the one he had expressed earlier. He makes 'a desperate tender' and, throwing caution to the winds, suggests a marriage on Wednesday in two days' time. On consideration he modifies his haste – to Thursday. The urgency is underlined by the fact that the wedding feast will be made only for 'some half a dozen friends/And there an end' (27–8), a rather different affair than a masked ball for the cream of Verona society. The audience is aware that if Capulet had clapped up a marriage with this speed earlier his daughter's life would be far less complicated and his lack of decorous restraint now makes tragedy more certain. This contradiction in his behaviour supplements that which we find in Friar Laurence's. Despite all of the Friar's urging of restraint and patience he is nevertheless the figure who enables Romeo and Juliet to marry within a few hours of their first meeting.

Another pair of scenes which have similarities in structure while differing radically in mood are the lovers' first meeting alone in the balcony scene (II. ii) and the last night that they spend conciously in each other's company. Both scenes involve secret meetings shadowed by fears of discovery. The Nurse is the figure used to interrupt and foreshorten the action in both scenes. In Brooke's leisurely balcony scene there is no immediate threat of danger. There are no interruptions from the Nurse. Shakespeare took over the incident but developed a rhythm and a structure for the scene which gives it the exhilarating, breathless thrill of young love. Romeo climbs over an orchard wall to declare his love to Juliet on her balcony. In the later scene he climbs down from her bedroom on their wedding night. In the balcony scene Juliet is evoked as the sun and encouraged to kill the envious moon (II. ii. 2–6), in the farewell the real sun with its envious streaks appears in the east (III. v. 7–8). In the balcony scene they argue prettily about Romeo's name and he is willing to deny it for Juliet's sake; in the later scene they tease out desperate paradoxes which would turn a lark into a nightingale. Romeo makes an extravagant declaration about his willingness to hazard death so long as Juliet loves him (II. ii. 75–8), but when he makes a similar claim later (III. v. 17–24) we are aware that the danger of death is very much closer. The juxtaposed word-clusters of light-dark images common throughout the play appear in densest concentration in these scenes. In II. ii *light, bright, sun, day, morning, morrow, dark* and *night* make a total of almost forty appearances. In III. v the same words with the addition of *lark* and *nightingale* make a total of close to thirty appearances. In the balcony scene time seems infinitely extended for the lovers until their next contact: ' 'Tis twenty years till then' (II. ii. 170). In the second scene there is an indication that time will be transformed because they have no clear knowledge of when they will next meet:

I must hear from thee every day in the hour,
For in a minute there are many days.
O, by this count I shall be much in years
Ere I again behold my Romeo!

(III. v. 44–7)

They no longer have the assured precision of contact – the hour of nine –
for Juliet now fears 'O, think'st thou we shall ever meet again?' (III. v.
51).

The scenes which are so full of cross-references in language are tuned
to totally different rhythms. In the balcony scene Juliet can go off twice
and yet return twice to linger with her new-found lover. In the farewell
scene (only one-third the length of the earlier scene), when the Nurse
interrupts there can be no lingering. Juliet, in II. ii, forgets why she has
called Romeo back and he is willing to stand there until she remembers,
but, in III. v, she must urge him to respond to the light with immediate
departure. Juliet wishes Romeo were her pet bird held to her by silken
threads even though dawn is breaking (II. ii. 177–82). Later on he must
escape at the call of the lark. Her initial jealousy of his liberty turns to
fears that he might lose it. In II. ii Romeo looks up at Juliet as a goddess
eclipsing the stars with her brightness. In III. v Juliet, looking down on
Romeo, fears that her eyesight is failing because he seems as pale 'As one
dead in the bottom of a tomb' (56). Juliet, the light breaking through a
window into Romeo's life (II. ii. 2–3), declares in another dawn at
Romeo's departure, 'Then, window, let day in, and let life out' (III. v.
41).

There is an obvious connection between the two scenes in which the
distraught Romeo seeks out Friar Laurence in his cell for advice (II. iii;
III. iii). In the first Romeo can scarcely contain his joy and his eagerness
to start a new life in marriage. The Friar tries to counsel patience and has
the leisure to make comic capital out of Romeo's sudden switch from
Rosaline to Juliet. In III. iii Romeo cannot contain his despair as he faces
the sudden end of his new life and the marriage he has yet to consum-
mate. The Friar must again counsel patience and is hard pressed to find
some hope, some light at the end of the tunnel Romeo now finds himself
in. In using the same locale and a parallel dramatic interaction, a
restrained man confronting one given to emotional extremism,
Shakespeare makes us register variation within pattern. The part of III.
iii where the Nurse enters with news of Juliet's woeful condition may
cause our minds to recall an encounter on an earlier occasion (II. iv) when
she first came to hear of his plans towards her young mistress. The

sadness and desperation of the last contact the Nurse has with Romeo, filled as it is with efforts to patch with cloth of any colour, reminds us of the gaiety of their first meeting when there was leisure for bawdy innuendo.

The two scenes where, within a generally similar structural pattern, the most complete contrasts in mood and effect are achieved are II. v and III. ii. There are such precise correspondences and contrasts of detail that it seems likely that Shakespeare kept consulting the sheets on which he had written the first scene as he wrote the second one. The shock which the audience feels in sharing the change in Juliet's destiny is the more effective in that only 232 lines separate the end of the first scene from the beginning of the second. In both scenes we start out with Juliet alone, musing on her urgent desire for news. In both the Nurse comes to her with information which, because it is already in the audience's possession, allows for a total concentration on Juliet's reactions. The news in one has to do with love and marriage, in the other with death and banishment.

An examination of the opening soliloquies in each scene indicates how deliberately the echoes and changes are orchestrated. Juliet's impatience at the dilatoriness of the Nurse and with time itself is the essence of both speeches. In II, v the slowness of the morning's passing is related to movements of the sun:

> The clock struck nine when I did send the nurse;
> In half an hour she promised to return.
> Perchance she cannot meet him. That's not so.
> O, she is lame! Love's heralds should be thoughts,
> Which ten times faster glide than the sun's beams
> Driving back shadows over low'ring hills.
>
> (II. v. 1–6)

At the opening of the later scene Juliet urges the sun to race into the west:

> Gallop apace, you fiery-footed steeds,
> Towards Phoebus' lodging! Such a wagoner
> As Phaeton would whip you to the west
> And bring in cloudy night immediately.
> Spread thy close curtain, love-performing night,
> That runaways' eyes may wink, and Romeo
> Leap to these arms untalked of and unseen.
>
> (III. ii. 1–7)

In the first scene the audience knows that Juliet's apprehensions are unfounded for time will speed her to the altar; in the second scene we know that time will speed faster than she could wish and take Romeo away from her. Her first invocation to speed touches on doves and blind Cupid: 'Therefore no nimble-pinioned doves draw Love,/And therefore hath the wind-swift Cupid wings (II. v. 7–8). In the second scene she refers to the blindness of love: 'Lovers can see to do their amorous rites/By their own beauties; or, if love be blind,/It best agrees with night' (III. ii. 8–10). An invocation to night in the later soliloquy (III. ii. 10–13) contrasts with a reference to the sun's journey in the earlier one (II. v. 9–11). Juliet impatiently refers to an absence of warm blood in the Nurse:

> Had she affections and warm youthful blood,
> She would be as swift in motion as a ball;
> My words would bandy her to my sweet love,
> And his to me.
>
> (II. v. 12–15)

In the later scene she refers to her own untamed blood: 'Hood my unmanned blood, bating in my cheeks,/With thy black mantle till strange love grow bold,/Think true love acted simple modesty' (III. ii. 14–16). This soliloquy goes on to elaborate more images of day and night and, in anticipating the death of Romeo, prepares the way for Juliet's confusion in the news the Nurse brings.

Upon the Nurse's arrival in the first scene fifty lines are devoted to her delay in transmitting the news (II. v. 18–68). Brooke has his Nurse delay the news of the marriage arrangements because she fears an injury to Juliet in a sudden excess of joy. Shakespeare modifies this effectively by allowing his Nurse, already seen as a figure given to self-indulgent jokes and long-winded stories (I. iii. 16–57), to tease Juliet mischievously and to hold back the glad tidings by pretending to be absorbed in her aches and pains. In the second scene the Nurse, genuinely distressed by the news she must impart, manages to confuse Juliet into believing initially that Romeo has been killed. This confusion occupies forty-one lines before Juliet understands that Romeo is banished for killing Tybalt (III. ii. 32–72). As we watch the genuine grief and emotional wrenching caused by painful problems of divided duty in III. ii, we are reminded how recently we enjoyed the innocent Juliet pleading with her crafty old Nurse for the joyous news that would change her life. To achieve this parallelism and contrast Shakespeare makes considerable changes in Brooke's account. In Brooke there is no scene of a distraught Nurse bringing news in a confused fashion. Juliet simply hears the news as it spreads generally through the town. In Brooke the conflicting strains of grief in Juliet are explored at great length (1075–162) but she is alone in her torment. Only after Juliet has swooned does the Nurse enter to try to distract her from her grief. Out of this major sequence in Brooke, Shakespeare not only created an echo of an earlier scene, he also, in having Juliet wrangle not only with herself but with the Nurse, prepares the audience for the later irrevocable split between them.

In each half of the play there are mundane, domestic details of the preparation of a feast at the Capulets. There is a brief prologue to the feast for the masked ball in the hectic racing back and forth of Capulet's servants as they try to cope with many guests (I. v. 1–16). There is the same brisk business of attending to practical details later when Capulet orders servingmen to hire twenty cunning cooks and worries about whether everything will be ready in time for the marriage feast of Paris and Juliet (IV. ii. 1–10). There is more bustle as the servants are hurried off on various errands on the morning of the marriage day (IV. iv). There is no mention in Brooke of hasty preparations for a marriage feast. The idea of echoing in this feast the bustle in the earlier one is Shakespeare's. At the first feast the killjoy Tybalt tries to interrupt the merriment. The second feast, prepared for a wedding, can take place only as a wake because the killjoy interrupter is now Juliet herself feigning death. The man who loses at both feasts is Paris. Each occasion climaxes in a discovery; Romeo learns he has fallen in love with a Capulet and Paris discovers he is to have no marriage partner. The smallest of details is made to serve the contrast. The essence of the masked ball is music and dance which Capulet eagerly encourages. There was to have been music at the marriage feast but, after the discovery of Juliet's body, Peter is left to ask for a woeful ballad and slow dance melodies which the musicians' sense of decorum leads them to decline (IV. v. 100–11).

There is a subdued connection between two scenes in which Juliet is presented in the setting of her own home for the first time (I. iii) and the last occasion we see her there (IV. v). We first meet her as she is being summoned by the Nurse to a discussion with her mother about a prospective match to Paris: 'Now, by my maidenhead at twelve years old,/I bade her come. What, lamb! what, ladybird!/God forbid, where's this girl? What, Juliet!' (I. iii. 2–4). At the opening of IV. v the Nurse calls Juliet to arise to meet her bridegroom: 'Mistress! what, mistress! Juliet! Fast, I warrant her, she./Why, lamb! why, lady! Fie, you slug-abed' (IV. v. 1–2). In the first scene with its gossipy, leisurely tempo and the Nurse's bawdy innuendoes the emphasis, in recalling Juliet's infancy, is the promise of life ahead of the girl. But in the second scene after only an instant of the Nurse's bawdy teasing the characters can look ahead only to Juliet's entombment.

In order to achieve parallelism and contrast Shakespeare made many important additions to the accounts he found in his sources and altered considerably the proportions and the weighting of the narrative incidents he found in Brooke, his major source. Shakespeare devotes more space to the initial meeting of the lovers, to their marriage, and to the circumstances which lead to their separation than Brooke does. In the first half of his play Shakespeare devotes a good deal of space to the Nurse, a character Brooke delineates in a dozen lines. He gives much space to Mercutio for whom there is no original in Brooke, and to Tybalt who appears in Brooke only to duel to the death. In Brooke there are no narrative details devoted to either Capulet or Paris until after Romeus's banishment. In Shakespeare Paris is introduced as a suitor for Juliet before Romeo has ever set eyes on her. In Brooke the idea of a marriage to Paris only comes to Capulet when he searches for some way of distracting Juliet from her grief over Tybalt at a point (1881) two-thirds of the way through the poem. By finding ways of filling out and inventing characters and details for the first half of his play Shakespeare gives himself greater opportunity to develop parallels and contrasts in the second half. By the moment of Tybalt's death in Brooke's account (1034) we are only a little over one-third of the way through his poem of 3020 lines. Shakespeare makes that moment almost the exact half-way mark in his play. Shakespeare altered the time-frame of his sources to put a more continuous pressure on his lovers. Brooke imposes limitations on the access the lovers have to each other but is by no means as severe as Shakespeare in the cruel gallop of events. After the masked ball Brooke's Romeus stands outside Juliet's window night after night for several weeks before they have a second meeting and agree to marry. After the marriage Brooke allows the lovers to meet nightly for two months before Romeus embroils himself in the feud. Shakespeare takes several details for his final dawn farewell from Brooke but he adds to the pathos by making the wedding night the first and last night the lovers spend together. Romeo has blighted their hopes by entering the feud even before the marriage has been consummated. The events to which Brooke gave much space and great detail are the ones which immediately follow Romeus's banishment. Shakespeare edits the material in Brooke very carefully, most especially in the radical cutting of the sententious speeches of Friar Laurence, without losing any of its flavour. In the dawn parting Brooke allows Juliet extensive expression of her fears that Romeus will abandon her, whereas Shakespeare concentrates on the lovers' anguish at the brevity of time available to them. The events which Shakespeare dramatizes in III. ii, III. iii, and III. v are taken from Brooke. In Shakespeare they occupy 382 of the 2993 lines of the play – a little more than an eighth. In Brooke they are covered (1051–727) by 677 lines of the 3020-line poem – somewhere close to one-quarter of the work. This switch in emphasis allows Shakespeare the space to develop material to supplement Brooke's account. Some of it produces the parallelism and contrast in events on each side of the turning point which I have described. Some of the changes in the second half of the play – the disappearance of a more fully developed Tybalt, the absence of the invented roles of Mercutio and Benvolio, and the diminished role of the Nurse – add to our awareness of the encroaching shadows of death which isolate the lovers. Shakespeare makes his acceleration of the fatal events the more unbearable by the echoing scenes in which the innocent hopes and joys that seem to promise a rejuvenation of society in a framework of comedy turn to the fears and anguish of an inescapable tragedy. Shakespeare signals that change by a contrast in the kiss which opens the relationship of the lovers and the kiss which closes it. Romeo, riddling wittily at the masked ball, comes as a pilgrim to a saint. Juliet restores him to faith from despair in a kiss which purges his sin: 'Then move not while my prayer's effect I take./Thus from my lips, by thine my sin is purged' (I. v. 106–7). At the end Juliet hopes to be purged of life by a kiss from Romeo's dead lips: 'I will kiss thy lips./Haply some poison yet doth hang on them/To make me die with a restorative' (V. iii. 164–6).

In both halves of this play, from the first kiss to the last Shakespeare gains a great deal of dramatic impact from his strategy of presenting the young lovers together on stage so rarely and, instead, giving his audience a multitude of scenes in which other characters are trying to arrange their lives. The effect of the sublime poetic arias in the love scene is so moving, the excitement and the tenderness of the young lovers so poignant that we might wonder why Shakespeare does not give us more of them and less of the irascible Capulet, the sententious Friar, and the gossiping Nurse, of whom we have more than enough. The answer is obvious. The brevity and rarity of the love scenes gives them a special power which is augmented by the contrasting ordinariness of the other events. Excellence needs the average for a framework, as Hal understands in the political manipulation of his image which he describes as 'bright metal on a sullen ground'. Shakespeare's telescoping of the time scheme of his sources down to a few days makes the vivid fire of their relationship shine the more brightly against the encroaching shadows of its end. In Capulet's tomb the lovers share the stage for only the fifth time in twenty-four scenes. Shakespeare here deliberately avoids the seductive possibilities of a final melodramatic meeting which any nineteenth-century dramatist, and certainly any opera librettist, would have exploited – Romeo, lingering in death by poison meets the awakened Juliet for extended 'addios'. He does after all, later on, undertake the dazzlingly audacious feat of bringing Antony, the botcher of suicide, by a deliberately cumbersome process, to the monument to die in Cleopatra's arms. Shakespeare even has the audacity to allow Desdemona some speech in a momentary revival after Emilia has arrived too late to save her life. But such a farewell would not have been to Shakespeare's purpose in *Romeo and Juliet*. The audience has attended to a sequence of events of wilful violence, blundering plots and accidents which have denied the young lovers all but a few brief meetings. It is consistent with our experience of the cruelty of time that they should even be denied the opportunity of sharing a few final conscious moments of farewell. Shakespeare does not, therefore, follow the example of Da Porto and Bandello in allowing the dying Romeo to speak to the awakened Juliet. He compresses the events of months in Arthur Brooke's poems into days but follows his example of time's cruel denial of a final encounter. *Romeo and Juliet* is almost 3000 lines in length but we see the lovers engaged in direct conscious interaction for only 280 lines, or under a tenth of the play. That Shakespeare allows them sixty more lines in the last scene when they are together, when they embrace each other, but when they cannot hear or respond to any words they say to each other, plays on an audience to the limits of its endurance. The irony here relates back to the meeting of the lovers at Juliet's balcony. The love between them is able to develop so swiftly because Romeo overhears Juliet declaring her feelings completely unaware of her auditor in the night air, a crucial detail which Shakespeare adds to Brooke's account. Juliet's involuntary delay in interrupting Romeo's final soliloquy before he carries out his sacrificial suicide echoes back to Romeo's deliberate delay underneath her balcony in breaking off her soliloquy too early. 'Shall I hear more or shall I speak at this?' (II. ii. 37). The love which was enflamed by an accident of overhearing is extinguished by an accident of not overhearing. Romeo's extravagant declaration of a willingness to die given so bravely in the balcony scene has become a reality. One of Juliet's first questions issued in the night air, 'wherefore art thou Romeo?' (II. ii. 33), expected no answer but received one. Her last question to Friar Laurence, 'Where is my Romeo?' (V. iii. 150), also receives an unexpected answer: 'Thy husband in thy bosom there lies dead' (V. iii. 155).

4 · 'What's yet behind, that's meet you all should know'

The structure of the final scene of *Measure for Measure*

In the whole canon one of the finest examples of Shakespeare's handling of a multitude of characters in a long, continuously unfolding sequence of action occurs in the final scene of *Measure for Measure*. The complex structure of the scene is developed around repetitions and variations in the pattern of events which have occurred since the Duke first made the mysterious declaration of his intention to leave Vienna. On Vincentio's 'return' the audience, in possession of all his hoarded secrets, attends with patient delight the various revelations which bring the characters to their own fullness of knowledge. The stunning impact of the scene results from the way that Vincentio's revelations are organized to produce a transformation in the characters and a promised renewal in society of a kind which even Prospero, with all of his magical powers, did not strive to accomplish. Shakespeare produced the complex alchemy of this scene because of the singular nature of the characters around whom he had developed his plot.

In the full spectrum of Shakespeare's characters we find at one extreme obsessive figures proudly wedded to inflexible principles in their pursuit of honour. Hotspur with his attractive vigour and Coriolanus with his cold, alienating obduracy are doomed to go down to defeat because they are equally incapable of adapting to alternative roles in face of political necessity. At the other extreme we find characters imbued with a cynical contempt for all principles who operate entirely out of pragmatic self-interest. The dedicated pursuit of a chameleon-like flexibility in role playing produces, at its worst, an appalling villain beyond all human sympathy such as Iago. But there is, too, something cold and alienating about successful, pragmatic politicians like Octavius Caesar and Tullus Aufidius. Shakespeare's most sympathetic characters are, generally speaking, those who are able to straddle a middle ground between these extremes. Rosalind, Viola, Portia and Helena display a flexibility in playing roles allied to a native virtue. Their facility in adopting disguises allows them to experience a variety of roles, to work actively towards their own happiness, and to rescue others from the sterile postures in which they have trapped themselves.

Measure for Measure, which varies so radically in mood, characterization and structure from almost all of Shakespeare's other comedies, has been attacked from a variety of standpoints as a 'problem play'. The conclusion most frequently reached is that it is a broken-backed affair, an amalgam of a convincing and gripping dramatic confrontation between Angelo and Isabella which veers off into the Duke's manipulation of mechanical plot devices of dubious morality to produce an improbable resolution. Shakespeare was not, however, afflicted by a sudden amnesia about how to sew varied elements into a coherent design. The play demonstrates how the comic structure, stretched to its limits, operates at the very borders of its legitimate territory. We are quite far here from knockabout twins, comic opera brigands, young courtiers entranced by the witty resources of language, young maidens ingeniously sparring with the attractive young men they are eager to marry, slapstick clowns and country bumpkins. In virtually all of Shakespeare's comedies there are leading characters and servants who win our immediate sympathy by their vigour, common sense, wit or grace. Vienna is such a society of extremes that hardly any character occupies by nature that middle ground which was for Shakespeare the source of harmony and fertility. Leading characters in many of Shakespeare's comedies often pass an acid test in giving and hazarding all they have for love and thereby engage the audience's full and unequivocal sympathy. Angelo and Isabella are at various times obdurate and inflexible in principle and so eager that others should give and hazard all that an audience's response to them and hopes for them are ambiguous until quite late in the play. The third major character, the Duke, seems by neglect to have allowed his society to sink into such complete decadence that all of his hasty plotting to patch with cloth of any colour strikes us as a difficult task he truly deserves. This mysterious figure undertakes a crash course of learning about the society which has flourished because of his negligence. Lucio and the low-life characters, Mistress Overdone and Pompey, are polar opposites to Angelo and Isabella in their openly pragmatic assumption that man's nature is entirely dominated by his animal appetites. It is often comedy's function to bring a fertility and spring-like renewal to an ageing society through the marriage of the young. It brings those engaged in unprofitable posturing out of isolation into the harmonious circle of normative behaviour. It is true that there are figures such as Malvolio, Shylock and

Jacques who are incapable of any fundamental change, but most of the major characters in Shakespeare's comedies of the 1590s have no deep-rooted resistance to or fears of change. In *Measure for Measure* Shakespeare posed for himself a significant challenge when he set self-righteous figures of very limited experience, firmly resistant to alternative viewpoints, in the forefront of his action. Vienna is a deeply wintery world where extraordinary efforts have to be made to produce the first signs of a spring renewal. There is no easy flurry of marriages here. The characters are taken to the very borders of the kingdom of death in threats of execution before they are recovered for life.

The play does not break into two ill-assorted parts. It builds logically step by step for four acts to bring the characters in a variety of ways to a point where they are ripe for a complete transformation. In the majestic organization of the final act the events in the first four acts, the themes, and the method of enforced changes in role are recapitulated. The pattern of the events is re-run at a jog-trot and the characters gallop through kaleidoscopic changes until they have been jolted into a completely new orientation. From the repetition of pattern emerges variation and revelation which, by producing flexibility in the characters, dispels the oppressive sterility in which society has languished. The last scene is structured as a trial, or rather as a proliferation of trials within trials. Much of the play has involved formal and informal trial scenes. The meandering processes of justice are examined in a comic light in the confusions of Elbow, Froth and Pompey in a hearing before Angelo and then Escalus (II. i). Angelo's interviews of Isabella (II. ii; II. iv) are full of the kind of eloquent intellectual sparring common in law courts. Claudio's pleading for his life and Isabella's condemnation of him constitute a kind of trial (III.i). In almost every scene of the play appeals for mercy are juxtaposed with definitions of the nature of justice. In a law court there are various distinct roles to be played – judge, plaintiff, defendant, prosecuting counsel, defence counsel, witness, jury and so forth. At almost every point in the play each character's speech, as they attack, defend, condemn, plead, bear witness, could be appropriate to one or other of these roles. The play is filled with situations in which characters have to confront challenging new roles from the outset when the Duke unexpectedly thrusts the burden of government on Angelo. The whirling of the characters in the last scene through a bewildering string of roles is a fitting conclusion to a story in which they have often been eagerly urging switches of role on other people while resisting any such suggestions made to themselves.

Angelo, proud of his invulnerability to the demands of the flesh, persists in judging all men by his own rigorous, ascetic standards. In the first half of the play the other characters are engaged in trying to persuade this inflexible man to project himself into another role – that of average, frail mortal. Escalus is the first to suggest that he should imagine himself capable of acting like Claudio:

> Let but your honour know,
> Whom I believe to be most strait in virtue,
> That, in the working of your own affections,
> Had time cohered with place or place with wishing,
> Or that the resolute acting of your blood
> Could have attained th' effect of your own purpose,
> Whether you had not sometime in your life
> Erred in this point which now you censure him,
> And pulled the law upon you.
>
> (II. i. 8–16)

Even though he asserts that he would expect the same severity should he err, everything about Angelo's manner suggests the man of limited experience smugly confident that he could never experience the role of condemned man.

The basic tactic Isabella employs in her appeals is to encourage the deputy to project himself into roles other than judge. Her initial suggestion is also that of an exchange with Claudio: 'If he had been as you, and you as he,/You would have slipped like him; but he, like you,/Would not have been so stern' (II. ii. 64–6). This fantasy scenario of a switch between judge and condemned man begins to have a horribly immediate practical relevance to Angelo when he discovers within himself a process akin to Mr Hyde's subjugation of Dr Jekyll. Isabella moves on to offer another suggestion of handy-dandy exchange: 'I would to heaven I had your potency,/And you were Isabel; should it then be thus?/No, I would tell what 'twere to be a judge/And what a prisoner' (II. ii. 67–70). The unstained novice, when she projects herself into the role of judge, is confident that she would be more flexible than Angelo. Her religious principles teach her to acknowledge the frailty of all human beings and thus she can project herself imaginatively into the mind of the guilty and recognize the need for mercy. The actor of Angelo must gradually make us aware, before he voices the matter to himself, that these abstract arguments are mirroring, in an uncanny way, his experience. She thinks to dislodge him from his firm grip on the role of unswervingly severe judge by suggesting more flexible substitutes. She is unaware that his hold at the edge of the abyss of sin itself is very unsure. Her next

suggestion of a substitute judge is a forensic salve rather akin to
accidentally stamping on the weakening fingers uncertainly clinging to
the edge of the abyss:

> How would you be,
> If He, which is the top of judgment, should
> But judge you as you are? O think on that,
> And mercy then will breathe within your lips,
> Like man new made.
>
> (II. i. 75–9)

Angelo the new-made man can only flinch in horror as she plucks him
from the judge's bench and places him in the dock next to her condemned brother:

> go to your bosom,
> Knock there, and ask your heart what it doth know
> That's like my brother's fault; if it confess
> A natural guiltiness such as is his
> Let it not sound a thought upon your tongue
> Against my brother's life.
>
> (II. ii. 136–41)

Angelo confesses to himself and to us that he is indeed a child of Adam,
but only when Isabella has left do we see how deeply he has submitted to
the full confusion of the handy-dandy world: 'O, let her brother live:/
Thieves for their robbery have authority/When judges steal themselves'
(II. ii. 175–7). In amazement he acknowledges the common bond he has
hitherto resisted: 'Ever till now,/When men were fond, I smiled and
wondered how' (II. ii. 186–7).

Angelo finds the purity he once prided himself on doubly galling when
it continues uncorrupted in the 'virtuous maid'. Hence, in the second
interview with Isabella, he tries to make her imagine an alternative role in
which she would have to submit to her own fleshly frailty. He follows a
circuitous path of shrouded suggestions, concealing as long as possible
any open admission of the new role in which he finds himself trapped.
The happiest solution for Angelo, we can guess, would be some method
which would get Isabella into his bed without either of them having to
acknowledge what was going on. His initial suggestion is sin by proxy
through an anonymous 'person':

> Admit no other way to save his life –
> As I subscribe not that, nor any other,
> But in the loss of question – that you, his sister,

> Finding yourself desired of such a person
> Whose credit with the judge, or own great place,
> Could fetch your brother from the manacles
> Of the all-binding law; and that there were
> No earthly mean to save him, but that either
> You must lay down the treasures of your body
> To this supposèd, or else to let him suffer,
> What would you do?

(II. iv. 88–98)

Whereas she had tried to draw from him an intellectual acknowledgment of man's vulnerability to sin, he tries to force on her an immediate physical submission to sin as her inescapable fate:

> Be that you are,
> That is, a woman; if you be more, you're none.
> If you be one, as you are well expressed
> By all external warrants, show it now,
> By putting on the destined livery.

(II. iv. 134–8)

But Isabella has had no traumatic experience comparable to Angelo's and so she has no newly aroused sensual being within loosening her grip on her hitherto austere identity. When challenged to submit to a new role she asserts ever more self-righteously her inflexible principles. We are given two glimpses of the varied roles Angelo will play in the final scene. When Isabella threatens to expose his corruptness he acts as witness in his own defence, asserting in a confident character reference that his false will o'erweigh her true (II. iv. 154–70). It is the last contact he has with Isabella until they confront each other again at the climax when the stage is inundated with assertions of what is false and what is true. By that time the stern judge will like an angry ape have played in the darkness such fantastic tricks that heaven alone can see. As a proud man dressed in his little brief authority he will strive desperately to prevent his fellow men from seeing that he is no better than they are and that he has, like the man he believes he has executed, some feeling for the sport. It is of crucial importance if we are then to have any sympathy for Angelo or belief in his humiliated repentance that the audience see him in the earlier sequences as more than a ruthless, conscienceless villain. The soliloquies which express his horror at his own sensual yearnings (II. ii. 161–87; II. iv. 1–17, 19–30) allow us to see him as a man overwhelmed in surprise at his vulnerability. Shakespeare ensures that we see him only a little while before his final humiliation as a guilt-ridden criminal desperately hoping to survive Isabella's denunciation (IV. iv. 18–32). But until that confrontation he has only played in public the role of judge; of the other roles available in a trial he has not yet played witness, counsel for the defence, defendant, or condemned man.

A significant aspect of Isabella's character throughout the play is her proneness to submit to authority. She can resist Angelo's authority because she is subject to the higher prescriptions of the Church's authority in her vows of chastity. But she is asked to behave as 'a woman' not only by Angelo but by her terror-stricken brother. In confronting Claudio's pleading she switches from the role of being counsel for his defence to being an almost hysterical counsel for his prosecution, asserting that such an abject craven cannot be her legitimate brother. There are limits to the sympathy for human frailty she had argued for earlier. Though in theory she had felt confident that she could 'tell what 'twere to be a judge,/And what a prisoner' (II. ii. 69–70), in practice she finds it much easier to be a stern judge than to project herself into the position of a condemned prisoner overwhelmed by fear. We are not asked to condemn her for her stern resistance to dishonour. But the violence of her response indicates how unwilling she is to question the precepts which regulate her life. We can understand her inflexibility yet, if we know Shakespeare at all, we can anticipate that it will have to be modified by the end of the play. In her uncertainty in trying to cope with this unfamiliar world of corruption she turns trustingly to the guidance of an authority figure. It is in these hapless circumstances that we have to understand how she can accept the Friar's proposal of the bed-trick for which she has been castigated by so many critics.

The necessity of flexibility in playing roles is usually demonstrated in Shakespeare's comedies in the most overt way by a central figure in disguise. We start out here with a Duke afflicted with a truant disposition; a ruler who, by all Elizabethan definitions, has been no ruler at all and has been derelict in his duties for fourteen years by his own count (I. iii. 19–31), nineteen years by Claudio's arithmetic (I. ii. 160–4) – 'a goodly nap' as Christopher Sly might say. To emphasize this neglect Shakespeare presents in Vienna a society more generally filled with decadence than that in any of his other comedies. We meet the Duke queasily leaving the dirty work of cleaning house to Angelo. On several occasions the Duke acts as apologist for Angelo's severity as a judge: (a) in his speech counselling Claudio to welcome death (III. i. 5–41); (b) in assuring Claudio that Angelo is only testing Isabella and is not serious in his licentious proposal (III. i. 160–9); (c) in justifying Claudio's execution to the Provost (IV. ii. 74–80). He is the only figure who has anything

positive to say about Angelo, though always for his own devious purposes, until Mariana speaks up in the final scene. We are never allowed to
forget that Angelo gets himself into trouble in trying to repair the
disarray which the Duke's lapses as a ruler have created. As the Friar the
Duke is constantly obliged to be a witness to the corruption in his state
and he is the most severe in condemning it:

> My business in this state
> Made me a looker-on here in Vienna,
> Where I have seen corruption boil and bubble
> Till it o'errun the stew. Laws for all faults,
> But faults so countenanced that the strong statutes
> Stand like the forfeits in a barber's shop,
> As much in mock as mark.
>
> (V. i. 314–20)

In one sense the play is the elaborately organized trial of Angelo, but in
another sense it is also the trial of the Duke. He counsels, comforts,
deceives and manipulates, and his interfering in everyone's affairs is
forgivable in one who has hitherto involved himself in no one's affairs.
He has no trouble in acting as counsel for the prosecution of Pompey
when Elbow is leading him to be judged by Angelo (III. ii. 17–37). He is
obliged to act as a witness for the defence as he endures all of Lucio's
slanderous implications that the absent Duke had marked criminal
propensities. A ruler who mysteriously absents himself from public
duties can only expect such rumours to attach to his name. In speaking to
Angelo at the outset the Duke, in fact, diagnoses his own past failings:

> Thyself and thy belongings
> Are not thine own so proper, as to waste
> Thyself upon thy virtues, they on thee.
> Heaven doth with us as we with torches do,
> Not light them for themselves; for if our virtues
> Did not go forth of us, 'twere all alike
> As if we had them not. Spirits are not finely touched
> But to fine issues, nor Nature never lends
> The smallest scruple of her excellence
> But like a thrifty goddess she determines
> Herself the glory of a creditor,
> Both thanks and use.
>
> (I. i. 29–40)

The Duke spends the play in a secret exploration of the damage which has resulted from his own failure to dispel the darkness in his society with the light of his own virtues. He has to construct a plot which will allow the fine spirits to be touched to fine issues. To assert that the pressure which the Duke builds in his plot is factitious because he could reveal himself and avoid all the manipulations resulting from the bed-trick is to miss the point of the play. The Duke is not involved in legislating his society back to health – Angelo has demonstrated the dismal consequences of trying to do that. The Duke wishes not simply to catch out Angelo but to change him and recover him for Mariana. He also wishes to change Isabella, as we can see from his refusal to inform her of Claudio's survival until the very end. If the Duke threw off his disguise before developing the bed-trick Angelo would be guilty, only on Isabella's testimony, of evil intent. But the lecher who reneges on his bargain to pardon Claudio goes well beyond the shock that he is, in his fevered imagination, capable of sin. He has to live with the belief that he has committed a sinful act, subverted justice, and shamefully concealed his criminality. Only when shame has done its work will he be allowed to discover that he is rather less of a criminal than he quite consciously tried to be. As the Duke stalks the borders where death threatens he learns a good deal about the value of human life. In orchestrating the final scene the Duke himself plays by far the largest variety of roles in it. He has spent his truancy accumulating experience in role playing and has been able to observe the tangles others get themselves into when they try to cope with roles they have not been prepared for.

The plot develops burlesque variations on the urgent suggestions the characters put to each other about changing roles. The idea of putting yourself in someone else's shoes as a broadening educational experience which can temper severe judgment is played out at the most literal level in the bed-trick. This is not carelessly thrust on us as an escape-hatch, a hoary old convention pressed into unsatisfactory service to shore up a creaking plot. Shakespeare is not an artist who accidentally paints himself into a corner. He invariably invents difficulties so that he can make telling points in getting out of them. He works out a precise logic for the incident. The Duke presents Mariana as poor indeed. She has lost a brother, a dowry and a husband. Isabella resisted Angelo's challenge to link charity with sin; but the charity she can show here is fraught with no danger. Angelo is a man who will go to any lengths to avoid a public, daylight acknowledgment of his true nature as a sinner. How appropriate, therefore, that he cannot distinguish one woman from another in the darkness. He has capitalized on the loss of Mariana's brother to avoid a match no longer financially advantageous. The dishonour he imputed to

Mariana he would now thrust on Isabella in forcing her to buy her brother's life. How pleasant to be able to force him back into the lawful contract he has dishonourably tried to escape. And, fortunately for him, in yielding to the tyranny of his flesh he wins a woman who can save him instead of despoiling a woman who has every reason to pursue his destruction. At the mid-point of the play we have a man who is determined to sin but is unwilling to allow any stain to sully his unblemished reputation, a woman who cannot bring herself to submit to carnal knowledge to save her brother's life, and a woman deserted by Angelo who finds that 'his unjust unkindness, that in all reason should have quenched her love, hath, like an impediment in the current, made it more violent and unruly' (III. i. 234–7). The characters, considerably altered from their originals in the sources, are carefully shaped to make the bed-trick an elegant solution.

Shakespeare never denies that characters can be influenced by abstract, rational arguments but he demonstrates far more frequently how they are changed by experience, the physical exposure in action which forces new viewpoints and alternate roles upon them. Such experience may be the result of elaborate plotting or of accident and both of these elements are at work in *Measure for Measure*. In the third and fourth acts devious plots and sudden accidents help us to see in different ways how flexibility or the lack of it in changing roles depends less on rational persuasion than it does on personal need.

While everyone else is feverishly adjusting roles Barnadine remains indifferent to prosecution or defence, salvation or execution. He has spent nine years in prison and has just been sentenced to death. When he is asked to submit to execution in order to act as a substitute for Claudio, he refuses. The Duke has made eloquent arguments and Isabella has made angry demands to the reluctant Claudio to accept the inevitability of death. Barnadine's refusal to go to the block because he has a hangover reminds us, almost at the level of parody, of the variety of responses men have to the threat of the grim reaper. When Ragozine's spare head becomes available to shore up the Friar's plot we see that diligent planning cannot ever quite dispense with accident.

It is not only the major characters who are relentlessly engaged in discussions about the nature of justice. Almost all of the minor characters speak up as apologists for laxity, the negligence in the application of the law as it has existed hitherto. Pompey, Overdone, Lucio and others all indicate amazement at Angelo's strictures. Most of the characters are obliged at some point to speak up as counsels or witnesses for the defence or prosecution of each other. When Pompey, as bawd and tapster, switches roles under pressure and becomes executioner's assistant we can see on the lowest level, as we see in Pistol and Parolles elsewhere, that with a flexible temperament there's place and means for every man alive. All of the elements, at the level almost of farce, help to prepare the ground for the revelations, the reversals, and revolutions in character which are packed into the last scene.

We can see how carefully Shakespeare worked out his coherent design if we note the significance of the many changes he made in the source material that he used. All of the changes enabled him to deepen the implications of the story so that the characters, involved in more complex events, are subjected to much more pressure to change. The alterations make possible the ebb and flow of fortunes in the remarkable scene with which he concluded the play, a scene which is in all but a few details entirely his own invention.

In Giraldi Cinthio's story of Epitia in the *Hecatommithi* Maximian, who appears only at the opening and close of the story, reigns happily over the Roman Empire through his deputies in various regions. There is no sign in him of a taste for 'the life removed'. The deputy, Juriste, is not peremptorily abandoned to the burden of unaccustomed rule, nor is he presented as a man devoted to the protection of a reputation for icy rectitude. He has no apparent internal struggle or debilitating guilt about his submission to lust. His proposal of a bargain to Epitia is not tortuously periphrastic; he moves to it quickly and openly. He has made no proud assertions about his ability to judge others severely because of his own uncorrupted purity. The idea of catching a puritanical deputy in a heavily barbed cleft-stick is Shakespeare's invention. There is no figure such as Escalus to serve as a contrast to the deputy's temperament. There is no figure such as Lucio issuing comments on Juriste or giving confusing evidence about the licentious character of an absent ruler.

The key change which Shakespeare introduced, and which made it necessary to adjust many aspects of the story, was in the presentation of Isabella as an innocent novice about to commit herself, when she first appears, to the chastity of the life removed. Shakespeare makes her, as he makes his other two central characters, someone who has to be drawn out of a temperamental taste for aloofness. Because of their lack of worldly experience the problems they face produce changes in them that are far more extensive than anything Cinthio attempted. Epitia resists Juriste's initial approaches, but she is encouraged by him to believe that she will eventually gain marriage if she submits, and she is inclined to believe him. The relationship between sister and brother is very different from the one Shakespeare depicts. When Epitia explains Juriste's bargain to

Vico he does not plead in abject terror for his life. He believes that Juriste will marry Epitia and, in his mind, there is no serious dishonour involved. He is not in Claudio's position of having to ask a prospective nun to sacrifice her vows. Epitia has no very deep concern about chastity and family honour. She is attracted to Juriste and makes little resistance to Vico's argument that the bargain is a good one. So Cinthio provides virtually none of the character traits out of which Shakespeare shapes the conflicts that fill the second and third acts of his play. Because those conflicts are not resolvable in a direct way Shakespeare needed an ubiquitous adviser who can work out a plot to salvage the situation. The happy solution was to bring back his truant ruler in disguise. In Cinthio there is no bed-trick for there is no figure equivalent to Mariana, and Epitia is no novice in need of a substitute. Nor is there any ruse of substituted heads to circumvent the deputy's violation of the bargain, for Vico dies, as Claudio does not. Shakespeare, consequently, omits the most traumatic moment in Cinthio's narrative. The morning after Epitia has slept with Juriste she is called out to look on the dead body and severed head of Vico. The grisly scene tends to strain our belief in her eventual plea for mercy on Juriste. Shakespeare does not confront Isabella with any direct evidence of Angelo's violation of the bargain. Shakespeare does retain a severed head – that of Ragozine conveniently dead of a fever – but uses it to convince Angelo that he has violated the bargain. It is possible that the idea of a substitution to save the brother was drawn from Cinthio's play, *Epitia*. There, indeed, Vico does survive but Shakespeare makes the test of the sister's compassion more severe than that which we find in Cinthio. Vico is restored, forgiven, and married to the girl he has violated. Only then does Epitia appeal for her husband Juriste's life and the Emperor rather unwillingly pardons him. Shakespeare undertook the remarkable challenge of having Isabella plead for her enemy *before* she knows that her brother has survived.

Cinthio brings his novella to its conclusion in an orderly, straight-forward fashion with no surprise revelations. When Epitia reveals her grievance to Maximian Juriste is summoned and, after a mere gesture of brazening things out, admits his guilt. Epitia is never in a position where she can fear a miscarriage of justice. Juriste does not, like Angelo, dig a deeper and deeper hole for himself until he is completely crushed in humiliation at the revelation of his hypocrisy. Juriste thinks his troubles are over after the Emperor forces Epitia to marry him but is stunned to learn that he must pay with his head for killing Vico. Epitia then pleads for her husband's life and Maximian yields to her eloquent compassion. Though there is, in Cinthio's dramatic version, a sister, Angela, trying to enlist sympathy for Juriste, which may have supplied a hint for Mariana, it is important to remember that Epitia is unmoved by the appeal. If Shakespeare had wished to achieve Cinthio's simple resolution he could have had the Duke, as soon as he enters the city, indicate all that he has learned in his disguise as a Friar. That would have allowed him to dispense with just about all of the first 351 lines of V. i, and would have made unnecessary some of his continuing manipulations thereafter. In fact lines 314–20 with a few specific details and the amazed responses would have been enough.

Shakespeare used Cinthio for several of the basic plot elements but for hardly any of the traits of his characters. He may, however, have taken some hints for his characters from George Whetstone's play *Promos and Cassandra*. Promos is not suddenly burdened with responsibility for the King appoints him to serve with others, not as his substitute, but in a normal administrative capacity as his lieutenant. But there is in Promos some of the self-righteous severity we find in Angelo. When he is first attracted by Cassandra's beauty we see him in soliloquy horrified by his vulnerability and determined to resist temptation. Even so Promos is not quite such a proud, secretive figure as Angelo. He discusses his lustful intentions with his servant Phallax who proposes that the sister be made to bargain for her brother's life with her chastity. But Promos, like Cinthio's Juriste, does offer marriage to the girl if she will yield. Andrugio has some of the craven qualities with which Shakespeare endowed Claudio, but he has no impediment in pleading with Cassandra to save him. He is convinced Promos will marry her and so does not consider that the bargain will make any serious stain on the family honour. Cassandra yields to his arguments and voices her hope that Promos will find her attractive enough to marry after he has taken her virginity. There are, in Whetstone, low-life bawdy characters and they may have suggested a corrupt city neglected by its ruler for which there is no counterpart in Cinthio. Shakespeare's central device of bringing back his ruler in disguise to control the plot owes no more to Whetstone than it does to Cinthio. Hence Whetstone's resolution is not at all like Shakespeare's. The King comes to the city already convinced of the truth of the story Cassandra has told him. He does, however, initially play the innocent by asserting how much he has heard to Promos's credit. Those with grievances are asked to declare them publicly. Promos, when accused, admits his guilt but, unlike Angelo, he begs for mercy and shows no signs of being crushed by humiliation. Whetstone develops the resolution in several episodic scenes in which the comic subplot and the revelation of Promos's crime are mingled together. Promos is saved from punishment not by any pleas made on his behalf but because the brother, Andrugio, suddenly turns up.

Shakespeare maintains a dramatic tension throughout his play by making his characters discover in surprise strengths and weaknesses they had not suspected in themselves. By the end of the first four acts Shakespeare has lulled many of the key characters into a false sense of security as a result of their reliance on or ignorance of the bed-trick which allows them to believe that they may not have to pursue the consequences of their behaviour to a conclusion. The last act is set up as a minefield full of trip-wires in which the characters, jolted by a sequence of explosive shocks, are forced away from any reversion to an aloof inflexibility and into a new orientation towards their responsibilities to each other.

Act V, Scene i

Part 1	1–351	(351)	Part 2	352–534	(183)
(i)	1–18	(18)	(VII)	352–75	(24)
(II)	19–125	(107)	(viii)	376–95	(20)
(iii)	126–62	(37)	(IX)	396–451	(56)
(IV)	163–258	(96)	(x)	452–65	(14)
(v)	259–76	(18)	(xi)	466–73	(8)
(VI)	277–351	(75)	(XII)	474–93	(20)
			(XIII)	494–519	(26)
			(xiv)	520–34	(15)

In the following analysis I identify fourteen segments in the developing action of the last scene. The scene divides itself into two parts. The first part, which occupies two-thirds of the action, ends when the Duke is revealed beneath the Friar's hood (351). In the whole scene there are seven major stages in segments of varying length devoted to public confrontations, demands for justice, surprise revelations and pleas for mercy. Interspersed are shorter interludes which are devoted to the more mechanical needs of the plot or to more private discussions which stem from or have a bearing on the surprising public revelations. Thus the scene mirrors in little the pattern of the play as a whole which alternates major confrontations of character with the Duke's secret manipulations of the plot and his various conversations with characters such as Friar Thomas, the Provost, Barnadine and Lucio. I use upper-case Roman numerals to designate the major segments where some form of revelation helps to move the characters towards a resolution of the problems which have troubled them. I use the lower-case numerals to indicate the bridging interludes. The length in lines of each segment is indicated by the number in brackets.

Part I (1–351)

Part I is filled with angry accusations, Lucio's relentless sexual innuendoes, a series of judicial hearings in which the identity of who it is that is on trial is subject to continual change. This part is plagued by disorder in the various attempts to elicit and suppress the truth. The Duke departs (258) deputing Angelo as judge in his stead much as he had done in the first scene of the play. Early in the play Isabella had to make a plea before Angelo on the nature of justice as it related to her brother's case. As a consequence of her failure to prevail then she again finds herself a spokesman for justice, this time for the punishment of Angelo. Throughout the first four acts of the play we have found Lucio pressing himself in where he was not wanted. He is as irrepressible as ever. Early in the play the Duke had disappeared only to re-emerge as the Friar in his endeavour of catching out the precise Angelo. In the last scene he returns as the Friar engaged in the same task. So the first part of this final scene presents a state of disorder in which the righteous go unheeded and a corrupt judge conceals his wrongdoings – a clamorous dramatic shorthand with variations of the recent events in Vienna. We have been made aware of various kinds of society as the play progressed; one in anarchic disorder because of leniency and neglect; one crushed by the ferocious application of a severe and inflexible legal code; one which would pursue the revenge of the *lex talionis*; one which presents a surface order which conceals corrupt secret deals. The last scene presents us with elements from all of these – revenge, laxity, severity, hypocrisy, erring judgment – as the characters struggle to reveal and conceal crime. The major figures are at one moment vigorously asserting the guilt of others, at the next moment the subject of prosecution themselves. They are whirled through a remarkable variety of roles but they are all at some point placed in the dock as defendants and threatened with punishment for real or supposed crimes.

(i) 1–18

The re-entry of the Duke into his society at the city gates is faintly suggestive of a symbolic rebirth. His statement to Angelo and Escalus that he has heard 'Such goodness of your justice' (6) is akin to his confidence in their virtues when he first departed. Shakespeare emphasizes how little things seem changed from the beginning when he has the Duke reiterate the importance of not hiding their virtues, a point he made when he first invested Angelo with power (I. i. 29–40):

> O, your desert speaks loud, and I should wrong it
> To lock it in the wards of covert bosom,
> When it deserves with characters of brass
> A forted residence 'gainst the tooth of time
> And razure of oblivion. Give we our hand,
> And let the subject see, to make them know
> That outward courtesies would fain proclaim
> Favors that keep within. (9–16)

That, as the Duke well knows and as Hamlet would say, is 'wormwood'. In acting as a sort of character witness the Duke seems to use the word 'favors' in the straightforward sense of 'goodwill', the good actions Angelo has performed. Angelo in the ward of his covert bosom perceives in it, no doubt, another sense without realizing how clearly the Duke understands the appropriateness of that other meaning. Angelo has pretended that he would do Isabella a favour if she, with her body, would do one for him. There is a specific legal signification for the word 'favour' which is relevant here – 'partiality towards a litigant, competitor; personal sympathies as interfering with justice'. It is, as the audience knows, the most important part of the business remaining in the play to proclaim those favours which Angelo would fain keep within. In that process the Duke will reveal all the favours which have resulted from the way his own personal sympathies have interfered with justice and which he has kept within. The ironic shades in the Duke's speech thus build a tension which foreruns the 'more requital' (8) we expect for Angelo. This kind of requital, praise for good services rendered, is only a cover for the different kind of requital demanded later in the scene – revenge or repayment for an injury.

(II) 19–125

The movement towards that requital begins at once. When Isabella steps forward with her cry for justice the Duke urges her to 'reveal' herself, make a verbal explanation, to Angelo. Her accusation concerns Angelo's insistence that she 'reveal' herself to him in a much different sense. Isabella combines a number of roles. She is a plaintiff asking for redress of the wrongs she has suffered. In vilifying Angelo as a corrupt judge she acts as counsel for his prosecution in the role she had threatened to take on earlier (II. iv. 149–54). All of her earlier arguments for excusing sinful man are forgotten in her vehement attack on Angelo. She has already had some experience as a severe prosecutor motivated by personal grievance in her condemnation of Claudio (III. i). We can never forget that when we first met this woman she was arguing for yet stricter regulations in that strictest of orders, the St Clares. She has demonstrated at times the same predilection for stern legal proceeding which Angelo professes (II. ii. 29–33; III. i. 144–7, 149–51). Despite her appeals for mercy in recognition of man's frail nature her violent reactions to both Claudio and Angelo may have a common source – their suggestions that she has the capacity to be a mortal sinner. We cannot avoid noting that Shakespeare has arranged matters so that she has extensive interaction with only three men in the play. Two of them, Angelo and Claudio, try to persuade her that she is attractive, and a fit partner for sexual pleasure; the third, the Duke, will propose recovering her from a life in the convent for marriage.

The Isabella we meet at the outset of this final scene may not yet be ready to extend mercy to her enemy, but she is not the same woman we met at the convent (I. iv). In her public acknowledgment that she has tried to tamper with justice by submitting to Angelo we begin to see a potentiality for change. This confession, albeit to a sinful act she has never committed, is remarkable, for we must remember that, no matter how deep her trust in the Friar is, she has no guarantee whatsoever that she will be able to wipe away this public stain on her character. In taking the role of aggrieved plaintiff she has to admit to being a sinner. This admission of a frailty she does not possess before a man trying to conceal a frailty which troubles him allows us to make a connection between the two characters who were initially confident of their invulnerability. Her simulated confession prepares the ground for his eventual penitential self-abasement. The Duke listens sympathetically to her argument that Angelo should be placed in the dock but then feigns to find tinges of madness in her claims. He acts as a character witness for Angelo, thus fulfilling the deputy's prophecy (II. iv. 154–8), and proceeds to the assertion that she is a fit subject for prosecution because she is engaged in a plot (112–14). With the kind of harsh, peremptory justice Angelo has been so expert in, and on no specific evidence, the Duke has Isabella whisked off to jail. She entered crying out for justice but she exits as an accused prisoner.

(iii) 126–62

Two witnesses give conflicting testimony. Lucio questions the integrity of the key witness, Friar Lodowick, whereas Friar Peter asserts his trustworthiness but declares that Isabella has given false evidence. Lucio has served as a witness in a variety of capacities throughout the play. He persuades Isabella to be counsel for Claudio's defence (I. iv) and is a useful coach to Isabella on how to make an effective appeal when she makes her first approach to Angelo (II. ii). He is a witness who denies Pompey bail and concurs rather ruthlessly in his prosecution (III. ii). But the ambiguity and unreliability of his testimony as a witness is clearly laid down in the confident assertions he makes in the pretence of privileged knowledge. As a witness against the puritan character of Angelo we are liable to trust him (I. iv. 55–68; III. ii. 89–108, 161–5). He mingles these opinions with whimsical assertions about the licentious character of the truant Duke (III. ii. 109–73; IV. iii. 152–62). In the absence of any corroborating evidence we perceive that Lucio is far more concerned with giving himself an air of importance than he is with the truth. We are thus prepared for the variety of his specious and dangerous testimony in the series of trials in this final scene. A law court is a sort of stage and Lucio is a continual reminder of a problem that besets justice – a need so urgent in some witnesses of grabbing the limelight that it allows them to say almost anything. Lucio's relationship to the Duke follows much the same pattern as in the scenes they shared earlier. Vincentio, as the Friar, had the galling experience of helplessly enduring Lucio's lies because he could not reveal that he was the very Duke being slandered. Now, in *propria persona* as the Duke, he is hamstrung in precisely the same way because he cannot yet reveal himself as the Friar whom Lucio is denigrating.

(IV) 163–258

The Duke's response to the growing confusion appears to be a continuation of his irresponsible habits for he declares he will remain impartial. This Pontius Pilate stance is followed by his even more remarkable determination to allow Angelo to be the judge in the case in which he has already been named the accused (165–7). Mariana enters the play as a surprise witness and, like so much of the truth, she is veiled. She is the first of three figures who will only be recognized when they are unmuffled. Friar Peter brings her as a witness for Lord Angelo to prove Isabella's testimony to be false. In acting as a witness for his defence she is at the same time a witness for his prosecution, causing Angelo to fall out of the frying pan into the fire. She reveals his innocence of any violation of Isabella's chastity and his undoubted guilt in tampering with justice when he fulfilled his bargain with his affianced wife. In the confusion of accusation and counter-accusation, of who is being prosecuted and who is being defended, it is not surprising that the precise nature of Angelo's crime is, for a while, passed over. Mariana's evidence concerns only her own relationship with Angelo. She passes over in silence his bargaining over and toying with a condemned man's life. Her reticence is explicable not only in terms of her desire to win a husband but because, as the Duke earlier declared, she deeply loves the flawed man who has hitherto disdained her. The nub of the case against Angelo, the deal for Claudio's reprieve, is only stated specifically by Isabella (96–103). It is not mentioned again until the emerged Duke apologizes to Isabella for not having prevented her brother's execution (385–95). The effect of this is to make us realize how, either deliberately or accidentally, people can lose track of the main issue. There are so many competitors pressing forward for the roles of judge, witness and prosecutor that the original crime is as completely hidden away in the public trial as it was when Angelo performed it. If the Duke were not privy to all the secrets there is no doubt at all that the procedures of the law would fail to uncover the crime. Shakespeare gives us a view of the law similar to the one he presents in *Much Ado about Nothing*. Dogberry and Verges stumble accidentally on the truth about a crime in the process of pursuing personal insults and tangential issues, but they never fully understand the nature of the villainy they expose. In much the same way Elbow only manages to get Pompey and others caught because he is pursuing the side issue of the insult to his wife. Only Escalus understands the nature of the corruption he brings to light. The point of that early scene (II. i) is to demonstrate the patience required of a judge in sifting truth from nonsense in the evidence. As so often in matters of law there are, in this final scene, far more witnesses than are needed for any simple resolution of the issue. Witnesses are constantly nudging each other aside with alternative candidates for criminal investigation. The audience is freed from all suspense, in its knowledge of the Duke's total control, the better to observe what an imperfect instrument the law can be. Shakespeare provides the audience, as the Duke provides his subjects, with a very practical demonstration of the 'judge not lest ye be judged' theme which was tossed around with an eloquent and airy confidence earlier in the play. It is Angelo above all who refuses to learn the lesson and his response to Mariana's claim is to ask more assertively for the power of judge, 'the scope of justice' (232). The Duke accedes to his request, 'Ay, with my heart,/And punish them to the height of pleasure' (237–38), still seemingly willing to leave severe punishment to his trusty deputy. He indicates once again that Escalus should help out Angelo and departs. The whirligig of figures being subjected to accusation merely keeps pace with similar mercurial changes in the matter of who is to administer justice.

(v) 259–76

Until this point we have seen Escalus as a patient, flexible man who knows how to temper justice with mercy. When Angelo, impatient of the tedium of sifting evidence, had left him to cope with Froth, Elbow and Pompey, hoping that he would 'find good cause to whip them all' (II. i. 130), Escalus had found ways of giving probationary sentences which avoided severity. We see him also at the necessary detail of administrative tasks when he sends Mistress Overdone off to prison (III. ii. 178–93). In these same scenes we see him, in exchanges with Angelo and the Provost, as a sympathetic defender of Claudio, favouring compassion rather than punishment. We consider how differently things might have turned out if the Duke had not mysteriously passed over a seasoned veteran to depute a man of untested mettle. But when Escalus turns immediately, in this last scene, to Lucio as a reliable witness (259) for opinions about Friar Lodowick the audience is alerted to a vulnerable blindspot.

(VI) 277–351

The use that Shakespeare makes of Escalus is instructive. We might expect Angelo, who has so much at stake, to be the one principally concerned in judging those who threaten to expose him. It is, however, Escalus who claims 'The Duke's in us' (293) and undertakes most of the cross-examination. There is at this point no purpose in demonstrating what we already know so much of – Angelo's flawed nature. The audience is aware that his hypocrisy must soon be completely exposed. Shakespeare's aim is not simply to expose the corruptness of Angelo. This last scene is full of surprises not only for the characters on stage but also for members of the audience. One of the most effective ways of demonstrating human frailty in judgment for the audience is to have Escalus, a man it has been led to trust and admire, make an egregious mistake. Hitherto he has been a peripheral figure. When he gets his chance at stage centre where he can wield supreme power he too commits the errors which such power so often entails. Instead of ignoring Lucio as the Duke has done he relies on him as a key witness and, on no hard evidence whatsoever, joins in the wild accusations of the Friar.

The focus on Escalus serves another purpose also. Shakespeare is well aware that in the remainder of the scene Angelo has to be crushed by the discovery of his crime, he has to repent, he has to have others beg for his life, and he has to be forgiven by those he has injured. Shakespeare is going to ask a great deal of the audience, as well as of Isabella, in applying the virtues of forgiveness rather than the reflex instinct of punishment in dealing with the deputy. So he tries to minimize the kind of alienation an audience would inevitably feel if Angelo were featured prominently as the hypocritical persecutor of his enemies immediately before his corruptness is exposed. We have been made aware that Angelo is heavily burdened by his conscience and we will soon see him in such depths of humiliation that he sues for the release of death. It is possible, therefore, to see in Angelo's relative inactivity a man not complacently relieved that others will innocently cover up his misdeeds but a man in such nervous tension that he is too sickened by guilt to involve himself in further sin. This is a central problem of sub-text of major importance to any actor determined to make a convincing transition at the climax of the scene. The prominence given to Escalus's vehemence suggests that an actor playing Angelo can make use of Shakespeare's shrewdness and tact in allowing him space to build up to and prepare for the transition when all of his hypocritical pretences are exposed. We are more liable to consider the significance of Angelo's lack of experience when we see that a wise, old man like Escalus still has a good deal to learn about the hazards of making severe, foolproof judgments.

The Duke, in his reappearance as Friar Lodowick, experiences the changed perspective of a new role. He provokes Escalus by his assertion that there is no hope for true justice (295–301). He speaks in general condemnation of the corruption he has observed in Vienna (314–20). He has come as a witness to corroborate the evidence of Isabella, but soon finds himself placed in the dock, swiftly condemned and, like Isabella before him, peremptorily threatened with a term in prison. Escalus, enraged by what he believes to be slander against the deputy, the Duke and the state, resorts to the kind of severe punishment which had been Angelo's speciality. The Friar has quite deliberately insulted Escalus to show how much judgment can be influenced by personal irritation. The temptation to apply severity exists in all judges if you touch them on a sore spot. It is a situation which the Duke himself will have to face in handling his own irritable fury at Lucio's slanders. We cannot be sure that Escalus is vindictive in his judgment but we know that he is unwise: 'Take him hence; to th' rack with him. We'll touse you/Joint by joint, but we will know his purpose' (309–10). The evidence of Isabella and Mariana has been contradictory and confusing. His excuse for racking the witness can be based only on his trust in the probity of Angelo and his reliance on Lucio's frivolously vague and baseless slanders. Were it not that Friar Lodowick is Duke Vincentio the result of Escalus's balancing of the scales of justice would be the torture and imprisonment of the innocent and the freedom of the guilty:

> Such a fellow is not to be talked withal; away with him to prison. Where is the provost? Away with him to prison, lay bolts enough upon him, let him speak no more. Away with those giglets too, and with the other confederate companion. (341–5)

Poor Friar Peter is to be locked up and the description of Isabella and Mariana as 'giglets' indicates the comprehensive nature of Escalus's misjudgments. In this entire sequence Angelo is given only three brief interjections. We reach the nadir in the abuse of judicial authority when Lucio is encouraged to manhandle and mock the prisoners. It is time for the reassertion of wise, temperate government and so, appropriately, Lucio 'makes' a duke. This second unmuffling has a symbolic function beyond the revelation of the true identity of the Friar. In his return at the city gates there was, it seemed, no new-made man. Now when the hood, faintly reminiscent of the caul in a newborn child, is pulled from Vincentio's head, we have a transfigured prince freighted with valuable experience from the dark underworld in which he has sojourned. He is a man fully capable of acting as an agent of rebirth in those around him. Even though two of his subjects, Angelo and Lucio, have been given enough rope to hang themselves with, there will be no more deaths in this play. The play is shadowed from the outset with threats of execution and prospects of sudden death. The only death in the story is of a character we never meet, Ragozine, who succumbs to 'a cruel fever' at such a fortuitous moment that he preserves another man's life.

Part 2 (352–534)

The Duke's emergence causes a radical alteration for the other characters of the range of possible roles into which they can project themselves. It is now clear which characters are fit for office, which witnesses are reliable and which unreliable, which characters are properly accused and which have the right to seek redress. But the emergence of truth does not mean that the education available through trying on different roles and seeing the world from different perspectives is at an end. There are more surprising revelations to come and all but one of them, the survival of Claudio, arise out of the varied experiences the characters have had in the first part of the scene. The matter at issue is how justice should be meted out to Angelo (and as a subsidiary issue to Lucio). The Duke proposes to give measure for measure in the full stricture of the law. The audience is aware that Angelo cannot be prosecuted for a crime that he intended but never committed. But the characters have brought themselves to a position where their fate lies entirely in the generous discretion of others. In the first part of the scene Mariana and Isabella have performed roles which were designed for them by the Friar, yet those roles helped to prepare them and us for their transformation. Isabella has been a witness whose testimony was thrown out of court. In her pursuit of measure for measure she ended up in prison. In Angelo she finds a man so completely shamed that the prospect of life seems unbearable to him. Mariana has known what it was like to be humiliated when Angelo fecklessly reneged on his marriage promise and when she was threatened with jail by Escalus after he had repudiated her evidence. The Duke himself, even though he knew there was no possibility of his being punished, has been threatened with prison and the rack by the very man who, next to himself, has the most humane view of justice. All of these characters know in different ways from their own immediate experience how men can stumble into sin and how easily justice can wander into error.

The turning point completely changes the tone and the language of the scene. Certain words echo through the play – *justice*, *truth*, *falsehood*, *dishonour*, *mercy*. The highly wrought texture of this final scene owes a good deal to the recurrence of clusters of key words. It is significant that some of the clusters are prominent before the climax but then tail off in frequency. In the cluster *just*, *justice*, *justify*, *judge*, *judgment*, *unjust*, *injustice* there are over twenty occurrences heavily concentrated in the various trials before the Duke's identity is revealed. Similarly *wrong*, *wrong'd*, *wrongfully* make almost a dozen appearances before the turning point whereas *fault*, *faults* make a dozen appearances after the climax when man's fallibility is being stressed. In the struggle to decipher what has happened another cluster – *true*, *truth*, *truly*, *honest*, *dishonest*, *false*, *falsehood* make almost two dozen appearances until the Duke re-emerges at which point no further argument about what is true is necessary. There are over two dozen occurrences of the words *confess*, *confession*, *forgive, condemn, pardon* spread right through the scene. The key word *mercy*, which has been used many times in the play, first occurs in this scene in the Duke's speech (403). He uses the word three times and Angelo, who more willingly craves death, uses it once.

Understandably several of the characters become more reticent in speech. Even though two-thirds of the scene is over at the turning point there is still a very significant alteration to be noticed in which characters have a prominent contribution to make. Though Lucio speaks only in brief interjections as a tireless busybody he does have twenty-six speeches until he unwisely pulls off the Friar's hood. Thereafter he has only four speeches. He makes one fearful comment (356) and then is silent for 143 lines as the Duke unravels all of his secrets before he turns back to Lucio (499), the figure he has kept in the corner of his jaw, first mouthed to be last swallowed. The silencing of Lucio clears the stage of the gossipy slander which has infested it. Angelo is also reduced almost to silence. Of his fourteen speeches only three occur after he recognizes his 'dread lord'. We can grasp Shakespeare's extraordinary tact in handling Angelo when we realize that, though most of the scene develops around interpretations of his character, actions and fate, of the 534 lines of the scene he speaks only a little over thirty. Isabella, too, has been active in giving evidence but of her nineteen speeches only three occur after the turning point. Escalus, so prominent in trying to protect Angelo, speaks only two of his sixteen speeches after he has been apprised of his error. The scene so far has been a disorderly chorus of vehemently angry voices. The Duke stills the chorus and voices speak in modesty or repentance as pleas for vengeance turn to pleas for mercy. In that change in tone Mariana is prominent for she is the figure least vulnerable to a surprising reorientation on the revelation of the Friar's identity.

(VII) 352–75

The action focuses immediately on the transformation in Angelo's character. This man, who has been burdened by shame and guilt and wreathed in secret, deceptive roles, seems to find relief in acknowledging his sins humbly. He begs the Duke, who seems to him 'like power divine', for the ease of death. He has yet to discover that there is a justice beyond the measure for measure in which he has so ardently believed.

The organization of this final scene is a little unusual in the way that it shuffles the major figures on and off the stage throughout. Isabella was hauled off to prison earlier, then the Duke departed and re-emerged as the Friar. He was on the point of being hustled off to prison with Isabella and Mariana when Lucio accidentally 'saved' him. Now Angelo, who has been on the stage since the outset of the scene, is packed off to marry Mariana as soon as his duplicity has been exposed. There are eleven characters who have significant parts in unravelling the secrets in this last scene. Only one of them, Escalus, is on stage for the entire duration of the scene. The restless activity of entrances and exits gives a sense, initially, of confusion but eventually of the energy of a renewed society.

(viii) 376–95

The revelation of the Friar's identity can hardly induce the same kind of awe in Isabella that it has produced in Angelo. Claudio, it seems, has lost his life because of the Duke's bungling and his failure to throw off his disguise until it was too late. Isabella's first thought, however, is not of taxing the Duke with his mismanagement. She asks him pardon for any pains she might have caused him. The Duke offers the lame excuse that the speed of events outflanked him. The brief exchange has, however, a very important function. It becomes clear in Isabella's compliant acceptance of the Duke's explanation that she is not possessed by a hysterical determination to take revenge. Her behaviour is one more step in preparing us to accept her response to Mariana's later appeal. She has never given any indication that Claudio's crime is a mere peccadillo in her eyes; it is 'a vice that most I do abhor,/And most desire should meet the blow of justice' (II. ii. 29–30). And there is no doubt that Claudio is guilty as accused. We know also how much she is prone to accept authority. The Duke's explanation of the blessing Claudio receives in death (392–5), similar in sentiment to the long speech on death the Duke made to Claudio in his cell (III. i. 5–41), is along the lines of Church teaching, which Isabella would certainly accept, about the vanity of earthly attachments. The Duke has to find out if her earlier eloquent arguments about mercy will have any consequences in her practical actions, so he hastens to a ruthless sentence on Angelo.

(IX) 396–451

The role of judge which Vincentio takes is one that has become familiar to us in this play. The Duke's speech on measure for measure (396–412) deliberately recalls for us Angelo's earlier speeches on justice. This is Mariana's cue to come forward in the role of counsel for the defence in appealing against the Duke's peremptory sentence. The Duke performs the role which Angelo had taken with Isabella, the unyielding judge resistant to special pleading. But he is not an impartial judge who claims only to be a mere instrument of the law. He also acts as a prosecutor and defends Isabella, as plaintiff, against Mariana's appeals.

Mariana's development is one of the revelations of the final scene. The other characters, once so voluble and assertive, have been silenced. The docile woman we met at the moated grange comes forward now as a forceful figure. Until the final scene Mariana has spoken a total of twelve lines. She alone of the major contributors to the resolution has been given no opportunity to speak about justice or to practise in an informal way the roles involved in a trial scene. It is in her that the argument for mercy once more finds voice. Escalus, who had wished for mercy throughout in the case of Claudio, asks for none in Angelo's case. Angelo himself asks for the full rigour of the law. The Duke, determined that he shall have it, offers Mariana the deputy's possessions to buy her a better husband. We know that all the arguments of the play have lead us to this point. Is it possible that in spite of all the laws, theories, unwritten codes, and the more primitive instincts, that the value of a human life is capable of arousing compassion in the human heart to initiate a process of rebuilding a healthy society? In one assertion of compassion the characters can make good all the wanton self-interest which led Angelo and others into corruption, and Claudio, so it seems, into an early grave. But because Mariana's plea is motivated by self-interest it cannot be her appeal which will move the judge's apparently stony heart.

The only figure who can resolve the deadlock is Isabella. She has, earlier in this scene, briefly had the experience herself of being a condemned criminal. In that apparent miscarriage of justice she could have had no confidence that mercy would be extended to her. In counselling her to pursue revenge the Duke asserts that, by taking measure for measure, she can patch up her family honour. But such abstract ideas are not now important. Dishonour is evidently something that one can live with as Mariana, abandoned and rejected, has lived with it. It seems that all of the Duke's devious manoeuvres to save her honour have not preserved her brother's life and, for a long time in this scene, it looked as if the corrupt deputy would not be scaled. Many critics believe that Shakespeare does not offer any satisfactory explanation for the Duke's persistence in concealing the fact of Claudio's survival. But this testing of Isabella makes perfect sense in terms of her experience in the play. She has diligently followed advice. When she has spoken up and threatened revenge on Angelo she has been rebuffed. She knows that the truth would never have emerged without the trick of the Duke's disguise. She must now rebel against the Duke's authority and demonstrate in action those values for which she spoke so well earlier. The Duke encourages her, as he encouraged Angelo earlier, to be the judge in her own cause, and we know what dangers lie in that direction. The situation is a reprise of the appeal for Claudio. The Duke insists on taking Angelo's position. Isabella can, if she chooses, take on Angelo's role of stern resister of appeals, or she can join Mariana who is taking on herself Isabella's earlier role. Mariana had taken Isabella's place in bed, but she needs Isabella's help to save Angelo who is now in Claudio's role of condemned man. Mariana has been a sequestered victim and she speaks to Isabella not on the basis of authority but out of personal affection. She has moved out of isolation and has renewed her hopes of a future in the social world. Mariana's wisdom is not born out of philosophy or religious theory, rather it is common sense grown out of experience. Isabella has been trying to handle danger, death and dishonour with theoretical precepts. Mariana has come to believe that 'best men are moulded out of faults,/And, for the most, become much more the better/For being a little bad' (435–37). Had Isabella been able to say the same thing to Claudio when he was, in his fear, 'a little bad' she might not have been so witheringly self-righteous. Justice must be administered in the knowledge of our own frailty. Angelo has failed to do that, Escalus has failed, and it seems that the Duke is failing also. Shakespeare has shaped Mariana's circumstances so that they have some symmetrical correspondence with those of Isabella. Mariana was dishonoured when Angelo abandoned her but the bed-trick has made marriage possible. By a crucial change in his sources the same bed-trick has averted a threat of dishonour from Isabella. Isabella believes that, like Mariana, she has no hope of recovering her brother. She has nothing to gain from sacrificing Angelo. She has seen enough of those, including herself, eagerly acting as prosecuting counsel baying for blood. When Mariana makes three successive appeals to her and she remains silent we know that she is looking into her conscience. When she kneels down as a counsel for Angelo's defence, fulfilling the Christian precept of forgiving your enemies, we have the visual image of a new start for society.

Lucio, Pompey and others have talked a good deal about what is 'natural' – no matter what law, authority or tradition say, men's natural impulses lead them into actions which society defines as crimes. Isabella could never go to the extremes that these low-life characters reach in excusing their actions and we know what chaos threatens when appetite receives no check whatsoever. But Isabella's act of kneeling down is a shift towards central, humane values which the Duke, with great ingenuity, is trying to propagate in his society. The foundation stone of the new society was not, we now realize, laid down when the Friar was revealed to be the Duke. That revelation meant only that all the confusion of the *past* had to be re-evaluated. It promised nothing certain for the future. By pretending to continue with an Angelo-like severity the Duke manages to cohere in embryo the possibility of a new community. The idea at issue is a society in which we are members one of another. We may go carelessly without check until anarchy threatens or we may endeavour to punish society into a restrained conformity. The Elizabethans experienced strains towards both of these extremes and, as counsellors of the golden mean, began that long search in the west for a way of achieving stability whereby men could co-operate in the creation of a just and compassionate society. The Duke, in pressing revenge on Isabella, gambles that she will resist him and exercise her freedom. She not only responds to Mariana's pleas and yields mercy to the man who failed to yield mercy to her, she goes further when she finds words to explain Angelo's behaviour and acknowledges that her own appearance may have been a cause of Angelo's stumbling (439–50). But the Duke is not yet ready to drop his role playing. He has further revelations which indicate that no one is to be denied an opportunity of taking part in the new society.

(x) 452–65

The Duke's irritability and his arbitrary severity appear to grow when he discharges the Provost from his office for his part in the 'execution' of Claudio. The Duke sends for Barnadine, the man who survived nine years of his lax judicial system and who recently resisted his arbitrary attempt to execute him.

(ix) 466–73

Escalus who had, earlier in the scene, expressed complete confidence in Angelo now indicates to the deputy his keen disappointment. This allows Angelo to reassert his preference for death rather than mercy immediately before the moment when he discovers that his crime was, in a deeper sense than Isabella understood, a bad intent which must be buried but as an intent that perished by the way. Angelo is not in a position where he can have much to say but the audience does need to know that his shame is so deep that he has not simply sloughed his sin aside when Isabella has begged for his pardon.

(XII) 474–93

Shakespeare has to avoid the danger of having any of the loose ends that must be tied up seem like anticlimactic afterthoughts. He shrewdly has the Duke, before he settles Angelo's fate, deal with Barnadine – the most marginal of the guilty figures. Barnadine, the sinner of longest standing, unlike some of the more self-righteous figures in the play, makes no denial of the charges against him. But we know that his conviction was only upheld under Angelo's sway and we know that the Duke was rather cavalier in trying to relieve him of his head. The Duke demonstrates that a renewed society must achieve not only the re-education of an Angelo, it must also cope with hard cases like Barnadine.

Claudio has been a convicted man from the outset. He has tried through Lucio and Isabella to make appeals. Under fear of death (III. i) he tries to act as counsel in his own defence but recoils from his sister's fury and submits to a seemingly inescapable fate as condemned criminal. He reappears only sixty lines from the end of the play as a reprieved man not as a result of any action he has taken or of any of the arguments made in his defence but as a demonstration of the forgiveness which is being applied in a new and vivid awareness that all men are frail. When Claudio appears as the third figure to unmuffle in the scene we know that even though it is the Duke's deviousness which has preserved him there is a sense in which Isabella has earned his recovery as a recompense for her charity to Angelo, a generous measure for measure. In forgiving Angelo's frailty she has forgiven Claudio's and she has, perhaps, forgiven herself for her assertion that her chastity is worth more than her brother's life. The Duke seems to intuit some such complex connections when he proposes marriage to Isabella. Even though she was not called upon to sacrifice her chastity it seems likely Isabella would have needed to commit herself to the convent had her brother indeed died, if only to justify her reviling of him as a coward. Angelo had succeeded Claudio as condemned man and, when the third figure is unveiled to him, he sees that he can join him in the role of the man miraculously reprieved from execution. In his case cowardice inhered in his desire to die in order to avoid public shame, but Angelo will have to live in this newly dawning world along with other recovered sinners.

(XIII) 494–519

We have seen in many instances how often justice can be tampered with when the personal affections of the judge are directly involved. The

Duke has been rubbed the wrong way many times, and especially in this last scene, by Lucio. There is a logic about leaving Lucio's fate to be decided last. He is not a carelessly forgotten loose end. He has flitted about on the periphery without ever playing the central role of defendant. But because he has been as careless in sewing his seed as he has been in handling the truth he will, for a moment, have to undergo the role of condemned man. The Duke has been extracting mercy by pretending to demand severity. Lucio is the final test case in which we must see the Duke swallow his own medicine in a circumstance where it is least palatable. It lies within his power as judge to gain a sweet, personal revenge by ridding society permanently of the slanderous gossip who has been such a thorn in his side. His initial assertion is a testy insistence on severity: 'And yet here's one in place I cannot pardon' (495), and he proposes the kind of harshness which has brought Angelo low: 'Whipped first, sir, and hanged after (502). He proposes a fate he has revoked for Angelo – marriage followed by hanging. There is a testiness in all of the Duke's responses to Lucio's gossip which reminds us that, whatever image of power divine Vincentio may present to Angelo's mind, he is a man like the rest of us. The Duke never welcomed 'loud applause and aves vehement' (I. i. 70) but his anger at Lucio's jibes show that he is not wholly indifferent to public opinion. A ruler cannot run away from nor neglect any of his subjects, nor can the burrs that stick be legislated out of existence. To terminate the problem of Lucio in such a way would be to return to the sterile ground explored earlier. It is fitting that Vincentio's last judgment should be one which tempers the full rigour of the law and offers mercy in a faint hope of reformation in the least promising of his subjects. It is difficult to understand why so many critics have found the treatment of Lucio harsh and unsatisfactory. Under the rule of Angelo Lucio would have been executed. But the Duke indicates how necessary it is to deal even-handedly in justice by giving Lucio the same fate as Angelo – marrying him to the woman he has wronged. Lucio's slanders have caused no more damage than the crimes which Angelo intended. But Lucio's frivolous attitudes to procreation, his irresponsibility in regard to the truth and in his relationships to others, and above all the air of self-importance he repeatedly exhibits make his enforced marriage to Kate Keepdown an appropriate method of chastening his decadent nature.

(XIV) 520–34

The Duke has restored Claudio to Juliet, Angelo to Mariana, and Lucio to Kate Keepdown. His statements early in the play indicate a reclusive nature, and his past neglect and truancy seemed to promise little commitment to society. He ends the play by reiterating his proposal of marriage to the woman who so recently was about to commit herself to a reclusive community bound by vows permitting speech with men only in the presence of the Prioress. Shakespeare gives us no hint of Isabella's response to the Duke's proposal. A renewed society in Vienna is only in the process of formation and not yet an assured fact. But Isabella has already recognized that Mariana's capacity to accept a deeply flawed man as her husband has more value than the fruitless negation of human bonds which revenge would bring.

We may think at the outset of the last scene that all that is left behind that is meet the characters should know is the real identity of the Friar, the fact that Mariana substituted for Isabella in Angelo's bed, and the survival of Claudio. The exposure of Angelo's hypocrisy would swiftly bring the humiliation he deserves. The Duke is admirably situated to play the role of *deus ex machina*. Many critics have eagerly yielded to Vincentio the power divine which Shakespeare so carefully denies him even after Lucio makes a duke out of a friar. The role of irascible, vengeful duke which he performs is rejected by his subjects. At the very end of the play the characters are, with few exceptions, very different from the ones who greeted the Duke on his re-entry into Vienna. The action of the play is resolved in favour of life instead of death. The play is checkered by alternating appeals for life and death. At the mid-point of the play the Duke makes an eloquent speech to Claudio about the necessity of submitting to the inevitability of death. His society coasts along the shores of death's kingdom, but it finds the strength to resist the imperative demand 'Be absolute for death'. The various characters marooned in versions of the *contemptus mundi* stance – Isabella at the convent, the Duke in his fourteen years of the life removed, Angelo in his frosty pride that no carnal frailty exists within him, even Mariana in the moated grange, or Barnadine snoring lethargically in his cell – must somehow be forced into an experience of life, into new perspectives and challenging roles so that instead of being unattached isolates they can constitute a society. Shakespeare achieves this by repeating in his final scene a summary of the trials, hearings, roles, lies, false testimony and misjudgments of the first four acts of the play. Until the final scene the characters have confronted many threats of danger but they are convinced that they will not have to suffer the full consequences of their actions and they believe that they can survive without any radical modification of their convictions. After the Duke's return, however, the characters in the variety of their experiences in the confusing sequence of trials exfoliate more generous and flexible attitudes. The repeating structural patterns in the action evolve variations which lead to an effective resolution. What was 'yet behind' was that the characters had to come to know themselves and each other, had to recognize their own vulnerability, the sterility of revenge, and the need for the application of compassion in the imperfect processes of the law.

Part Two

5 · 'But when they seldom come, they wished-for come'

Interaction and separation in Shakespeare's drama

We can understand some of the ways that Shakespeare's plays achieve their effect by attending to the precision with which he works out the relative proportions in the human relationships which figure in the action. This is not only a matter of how many lines a character speaks. A play is organized around a series of relationships. Some relationships can be given a good deal of stage time to develop, others may be merely sketched in or given no stage time at all. We may hear about relationships and events in report, but a play makes most of its impact in the events brought to life on the stage before our eyes. Thus the relative weighting of material is of crucial significance. I am concerned here with what I call the 'stage-life' of the characters, with how much of the play they are physically in the presence of the audience, with what proportions of the play are devoted to the various relationships.

In exploring Shakespeare's handling of the stage-life of the various relationships within a play I have been involved with a good deal of counting of lines, which might seem to be the occuption of a noodle. I am not trying to reduce Shakespeare's art to a mathematically accurate formula. It is not the precise number of lines I wish to focus on. The vagaries of lineating and variations in the texts make precision, in any case, impossible, so my numbers are usually rounded off and approximate. I use the figures mainly to establish the proportions within a play, to illustrate how much stage-life Shakespeare devotes to one relationship compared to another, or for what proportion of a play Shakespeare chooses to keep characters out of each other's presence. How often a character is to be brought on stage and which characters he is to interact with are the basic questions any dramatist must ask himself in building the scenic structure of his play. A constant aspect of Shakespeare's dramatic method is the development of plots which involve a separation of the major characters. Since separation is a primary motif of the romance form and romance is a major influence on this drama, it is not surprising that it is an element in a large proportion of his plays. It is his varied skills in using the separation of characters to his advantage that I wish to examine. Seen from this point of view it could be argued that part of Shakespeare's success comes from the scenes he chooses *not* to write.

I am not suggesting that there is a simple equation between the amount of lines a character speaks or the amount of time he is on stage and the importance of such a character in the eyes of the audience. Shakespeare can draw as much significance from having a character on stage saying little and taking relatively little action as he can from a character dominating our attention with his speech. A vivid example of this occurs in the deposition scene of *Richard II* (IV. i). The entire focus of attention in the lines of the scene where Richard yields up his crown to Bolingbroke (162–318) is on the King's imaginative ingenuity in teasing out the tormenting significance in his changed fortunes. Of the 157 lines of this interaction Richard speaks 133 and Bolingbroke a mere eleven. Yet his lion's share of the lines serves to emphasize how, in his poetry, Richard retains only a shadow of power while all the substance of political power passes to Bolingbroke, his almost silent opponent. This is in line with Shakespeare's whole development of the relationship between the two men. Because the audience knows the story and its outcome it anticipates the return of Bolingbroke from exile to seize the crown from the moment he is banished. He reappears on the stage in II. iii at a point where much more than half of the play's lines are to come. In the 1653 lines to the end of the play the two men share the stage for a little over 300 of them. What is remarkable is that all the complex manoeuvring of taking over the kingdom and then the transferring of the crown is conducted almost entirely through intermediaries. In the whole sequence of Richard's shifting moods and his voluble lamentations, Bolingbroke, after his return from exile, speaks a total of fifteen lines, a few dozen words, to the king he deposes.

The ghost of Hamlet's father has a significantly determining effect on the action of the play out of all proportion to the number of lines he speaks in the wide separation of the occasions on which he appears on stage. Towards the end of *Julius Caesar* the ghost of Caesar, in only brief flickering appearance, seems to have more power to affect events than the real Caesar had at the outset. Shakespeare often produces in his plays, in a few lines of poetry, an effect more vivid and emotionally moving than whole scenes of action elsewhere in the play. A skilled actor with a mere handful of lines can make a very powerful impression. I have seen Silence played so cleverly in *2 Henry IV* that he was the focus of attention whenever he came on stage. Yet in spite of all these caveats it remains true that the proportions of lines given to various actions and relationships is a determining factor in their effect upon an audience. If the focus of the story is on the relationship of character A to character B then the amount of time the audience observes them in direct interaction is of key significance. Of equal importance is the proportion of the play's running time that is devoted to that direct interaction compared to the other relationships the characters develop. It may be that A and B's story of its very nature involves very few meetings, or it may be Shakespeare's choice to develop a relationship by indirect action through intermediaries C, D, E, etc., relationships that occupy most of the play's running time. In sewing various plots together, inventing new characters, or in altering the time frame, Shakespeare is not simply filling out a two-hour entertainment or making its action more plausible, he is finding the most effective way of framing a story that had attracted him so that he might maximize its impact. One of the key elements in his strategy developed out of his understanding of how much interest can be generated in a relationship where characters meet rarely and briefly.

We can see Shakespeare's mastery of the mechanics of separation at its most basic level in one of his earliest plays, *The Comedy of Errors*. He strings out a plot for two hours by the simple device of allowing two sets of twins to wander through the same town, yet ensuring that they never meet their mirror images in the same scenic frame until they are driven almost mad by the confusion. Shakespeare's skill in ringing the changes on the device of disguise to keep characters separate, holding off the desired union of marriage, is a major aspect of his comic plotting. But out of this almost mechanical device he developed a skill in exploiting the psychological effects of separating characters from each other and from the audience. The most familiar example of this technique is the 'rest' provided for his tragic heroes – Romeo, Macbeth, Hamlet, Lear – often in Act IV, when an absence from the stage builds up anticipation of their re-emergence to confront the problems awaiting them. Hamlet, for example, during his sea voyage and rescue by pirates is absent from the stage for 500 lines. But his return to Denmark is anticipated half way through this sequence in the letter to Horatio.

Shakespeare indicates an understanding of the tactical use which can be made of limiting a character's stage-life at the very outset of his career. When he set himself the task of organizing the rambling chronicle events of Henry VI's reign into three plays, Shakespeare had not yet developed to any considerable degree the skill of showing how a character grows and changes in time in response to a chain of events. He organized two strands of action to illustrate the long nightmare that England endured. On the one hand we have a herd of competing barons, conniving, arguing, eternally realigning themselves. Their insatiable appetite for violent activity inundates the stage with blood. The faces in the herd, because of treachery and murder, keep changing but the activity is always the same, the urgent need to dominate the kingdom. Set against this changeable herd is the lone figure, Henry VI, on whose consistently inept political behaviour their activity is predicated. He is a shadowy figure, prominent almost by his absence. He makes virtually no decisions and merely endures while the barons take his realm away from him or give it back to him. His role as bystander is confirmed most vividly in the emblematic scene played out before him of sons and fathers killing each other (*3 Henry VI*, II. v). It is the way that Shakespeare organizes Henry's appearances on stage which reminds us how much England's fate is tied to its helpless, ineffectual king. Over half of the first play is devoted to the baronial squabbles during the protectorship before Henry makes his first appearance. He has been an apprentice bit-player in the realm for so long that he is never taught and never develops the skills of dominating the stage. For the rest of his career we have a varied study of a non-political nature. If he is present when important matters are to be decided Shakespeare gives him very few lines to speak. His marginality is emphasized the more in that he is given many more lines when trivial matters are at issue. But increasingly towards the end of the second part, when the Cade rebellion threatens, and in the last play of the trilogy, Henry is simply pushed off the stage and into the tiring house. Sequences of several hundred lines pass in which he never appears before the audience. His brief appearances indicate the power vacuum which others are so desperately eager to fill. Shakespeare does not need to give us many examples of Henry's ineptitude. By simply keeping him off stage out of the audience's sight he can give us a clear sense of the ship of state adrift without a pilot amid a sea of rocks and sharks. If we take the three plays as one huge epic of Henry's reign we can, simply in the proportions of the plays, see how much Shakespeare decided to interpret it as a half-voluntary truancy. Of the eighty scenes into which he divides the action Henry appears in only twenty-two. Of the over 8500 lines of the plays Henry is on stage for a good deal less than a third of the action. When he is present he scarcely ever has a dominant share of the lines. He has in the three plays a little more than 800 lines of speech, something less than a tenth of the material devoted to the events of his reign. Nearly 150 of his lines, mostly in soliloquy, occur in two scenes of the last play (II. v; III. i) at a low ebb in his fortunes. As a point of comparison we can note that when Richard Gloucester becomes prominent he speaks, in *3 Henry VI* alone, half as many lines as Henry has in the whole trilogy.

It is not only Henry VI's frequent absences from the stage which contribute to our sense of his weakness. Whenever he is on stage he is being manipulated by others. He has no skill in gauging his public appearances to gain maximum effect. Just as the love between characters becomes intensified by the rareness of the occasions on which they can express it to each other, or as a reconciliation becomes the more moving the longer it is held off, so may a king gain power by being niggardly of his presence. Shakespeare had considered deeply the proposition that familiarity breeds contempt. Hamlet expresses contempt for Claudius's public exhibitions of revelry; Octavius Caesar is irritated by the public shows those two great theatrical stagers, Antony and Cleopatra, put on; Timon makes himself too generally available. It is possible also to err too much in the other direction. Coriolanus can never successfully stage himself before the sweaty multitude. Prospero isolated in his library and Vincentio in his love of the life removed allow, by their negligence, corruption to breed in their societies. It is important in government, as in so many matters, to get the balance just right.

Everywhere in Shakespeare's work we find his keen awareness of the rules of decorum, of the virtues of restraint and the perils in overdoing things. Philostrate urges that a play should not be seen, for though it is only ten words long, it is ten words too long. He knows what is apt and fitting. Shakespeare's characters often censure themselves in mid-flight. Hamlet says 'Something too much of this' in his eulogy to Horatio, reins himself in with 'Why, what an ass am I!' when he falls to cursing like a very drab. Othello on being reunited with Desdemona in Cyprus feels 'it is too much of joy', and when he says 'I prattle out of fashion, and I dote/In mine own comforts' the audience is soon to feel how rare are further opportunities for him to prattle thus. Though the audience might be happy to have too much of a good thing, Shakespeare is wise enough not to give it to them and that shrewd restraint is part of the explanation for Mercutio's death, for the Fool's disappearance in *King Lear*, and Falstaff's absence in *Henry V*. Shakespeare ensures that his sparkling lovers Beatrice and Benedick, Petruchio and Kate, Rosalind and Orlando have to press in with the other country copulatives. He expresses very clearly the importance of balance and decorum in drama in the advice he has Hamlet give to the players. The disproportionate amount of time and attention clowns grab for themselves with excessive antics injures the design of the play. It is the judicious one must try not to grieve. There may be whole theatres of others who will applaud things 'overdone or come tardy off' but they must be resisted. Hamlet emphasizes here the importance of balance, neither too much nor too little, and tempo. The balance, the sense of how much is enough, is achieved in a variety of ways in organizing a play effectively. As I have indicated Shakespeare spent many years in his history plays examining the ways that kings tried, but most often failed, to get the balance right in governing the English people.

Henry IV talks a good deal about how much and in what manner a king should present himself before his people. He twits Hal because, like Richard II, he makes himself too frequently available. He indicates how much power a leader can gain by limiting his public appearances:

> My presence, like a robe pontifical,
> Ne'er seen but wond'red at; and so my state,
> Seldom, but sumptuous, showed like a feast
> And won by rareness such solemnity.
>
> (III. ii. 56–9)

From the outset we know that Hal is working on an even more sophisticated version of role playing. He features himself in the role of madcap Prince the better to set off his intended transformation into responsible heir-apparent when the time is ripe:

> If all the year were playing holidays,
> To sport would be as tedious as to work;
> But when they seldom come, they wish'd-for come,
> And nothing pleaseth but rare accidents.
>
> (I. ii. 192–5)

The 'rare accident' which Hal is quite consciously calculating and which will involve 'Redeeming time when men think least I will' (I. ii. 205) is thus prophesied some 300 lines into the play. Hotspur can bask in public glory the better that his plucked plumes can honour Hal's triumph when he slays the northern youth 120 lines from the end of the play.

In the sources of *1 Henry IV* there is no indication that Hal and Hotspur ever met and only a vague, ambiguous sentence in Holinshed to indicate that they might have fought in battle at Shrewsbury. Shakespeare structures his action very carefully to culminate in their confrontation. Since the characters are on different sides they can be kept apart by the exigencies of plot. The rebel and the madcap Prince can hardly be expected to find occasion to chat about common interests. So we see Hotspur at work in rebellion and Hal at play in the tavern. But because Shakespeare intends their eventual clash in combat to determine England's future he prepares for his climax throughout. The King compares the two youths and wishes they had been exchanged in their cradles (I. i). The Prince undertakes a parody of Hotspur's breakfast behaviour in the jesting at the Boar's Head tavern (II. iv). The King compares Hal to Richard II and Hotspur to his younger self in censuring his son for his truant ways, and Hal indicates that Hotspur is merely his factor to 'engross up glorious deeds' on his behalf (III. ii). Hotspur speaks mockingly of the Prince while Vernon eulogizes a seemingly new-minted hero (IV. i). Hal makes an offer to fight Hotspur in single combat (V. i) and Worcester reports the challenge to Hotspur (V. ii). Shakespeare thus devotes almost 250 lines of his play to specific comparisons of the two, or to comments by one on the other, without bringing them on stage in the same scenic frame. Hal, of course, does not share the stage with the King, the leader of his own side, until the play is half over (III. ii). But it could be argued that at any point after he has shown his true colours to his father Hal could be brought on stage to confront Hotspur in the diplomatic skirmishes which precede battle. After the interview with the King eight scenes occur before the two do meet (V. iv), and either Hal or Hotspur appears in all but one of them. The relationship is developed through intermediaries. Even in the battle itself Shakespeare holds them apart as long as possible by presenting a series of combats, comic and serious, between Douglas and Blunt, the Prince censuring Falstaff, the King confronting Douglas, the Prince fighting off Douglas. When Hotspur and Hal do finally appear together Shakespeare does not focus a singular concentration on them, for Falstaff lumbers on and, attacked by Douglas, plays dead. By storing up dramatic tension in the development of their indirect relationship throughout the play he can punch home the more effectively the brevity of their actual meeting. While alive they share the stage for twenty-seven lines. Hal adds fifteen more lines of commentary on Hotspur's corpse. Shakespeare does not choose to interrupt the chaotic flow of war by having them harangue each other in long battle speeches. The swift conclusion to the relationship also underlines what we have come to see as the inevitability of Hotspur's failure. Shrewsbury is not the chivalric field of honour he had antici-pated. It is haunted by counterfeit kings and a fat rogue who tempers valour with discretion. Hotspur, who would have plucked bright honour from the pale-faced moon, is swiftly reduced to food for worms. Shakespeare proceeds to devote considerably more time to Falstaff's ignominious battle with and claims of reward for the dead Hotspur than he has given to Hal's triumph over the live one. The dramatic weighting of the episodes reinforces our awareness of how outmoded Hotspur's ideas are. It makes it clear that though Hal has rid the state of one danger, there is still another, 'the strangest fellow', alive to deal with.

In *Twelfth Night* we have a physical separation between Orsino and Olivia which is not entirely dictated by plot requirements. In one of the sources, Barnaby Riche's story of Apolonius and Silla, the weighting of relationships is very different. A third of the story is devoted to an interview between the Duke, Julina (Olivia's prototype) and Silla (Viola's prototype) as they try to sort out the complications they have fallen into. Shakespeare took the hint for his separation of Orsino and Olivia from *Gl' Ingannati*. In that play the prototypes of Orsino and Olivia never meet at all, nor for that matter are the twins ever brought on stage together. Shakespeare gains considerable dramatic advantage from delaying until the very end any shared on-stage life to Orsino and Olivia. This separation does not so much make Orsino's love seem rarefied and ethereal, it makes it seem ludicrous, feeding, as it does, on no actual substance but on the self-indulgence of a fevered imagination. We feel this the more so because Orsino is set against others smitten by love in affairs which are developed vividly in face-to-face interactions. Viola seems to fall in love with Orsino at first sight, Olivia catches the plague at once when she meets Caesario and ensures that 'he' is in her presence as often as possible. Even Malvolio, absurd though he may seem, does have physical access to the lady his ambition pursues. In contrast Orsino's sighs, his renewed embassies, his theories about love, seem vain and airy trifles. Orsino, who pursues Olivia ardently throughout without gaining any access to her, is superseded by Sebastian who has never pursued her but who can walk in off the street and become betrothed to her in a trice. That leaves only one lover as completely out of touch with the object of his desire as Orsino – Sir Andrew Aguecheek. Before the final scene he appears twice briefly on stage with Olivia (III. i; IV. i), but he is merely a bystander and exchanges no words with her. No matter how much money he pours out to Sir Toby in pursuit of Olivia he never has the slightest hope of winning her. In the entire play he shares the stage with her for only fifty lines. He is a debased figure, a parody of a courtier, yet we should not miss the point that the courtier he is a parody of is, in part, Count Orsino. In the last scene Sir Andrew comes into Olivia's presence only a little after the Duke and she asks him how he came by his bloody coxcomb. For all his pains he receives from her mouth a total of nine words. But Sir Andrew, though his suit is as unsuccessful as Orsino's, has at least suspected that Caesario is his rival and has been involved in the comic complications of a mock duel for his love. He has had a closer touch with the physical reality of the situation than Orsino, or Olivia for that matter, ever have. Olivia, so vigorous in her denial of access to the Duke, finds that she is married to a total stranger. Where in *1 Henry IV* Shakespeare developed considerable substance in a relationship between characters who meet only briefly at the end, in *Twelfth Night* he shuttles intermediaries back and forth between two characters he keeps apart only to demonstrate when they finally meet that there has never been any substance to the relationship at all.

Much Ado About Nothing is developed around a somewhat different process of separation. Hero and Claudio spend a good deal of time in each other's presence but so rarely speak to each other that they have only the sketchiest of relationships. The courting of Hero, the wooing by proxy, arrangements made by the older generation with the lady having no very great say in the matter correspond to sixteenth-century circumstances rather more closely than do many of the marriages in Shakespeare's other comedies. The meekness and fading-into-the-wallpaper quality of Hero is Shakespeare's invention. In virtually all of the possible sources the equivalent figures to Hero are stronger and more voluble. In Bandello, for example, Fenicia is given by far the longest speech in the novella and much space is devoted to the delineation of her character. From the outset Shakespeare conceives of Hero as a shy figure dominated by her volatile father, Leonato. Critics generally try to explain away the easy manner in which Claudio is persuaded to believe that Hero is false to him, and his subsequent rejection of her in church, as conventions of romance that we must take for granted. Shakespeare, however, makes an improbable source-story acceptable by presenting to his audience lovers who are given scarcely any opportunity to gain a knowledge of each other. Claudio's inexperience and gullibility are outlined by the way he can initially believe that Don Pedro is wooing Hero for himself. Don John's second clumsy plot can work because of the severe limitations Shakespeare imposes in the on-stage life of the young lovers. Though Hero is on stage for some 970 lines in six scenes she speaks a total of 129 lines in the play and seventy-eight of those occur in the only scene in which she is prominent – the gulling of Beatrice in hiding. To Claudio she speaks a total of fourteen lines. We are told in an early meeting (II. i) that she is whispering to him, but the first time we actually *hear* her speaking to him is when she responds to his rejection of her on the marriage day (IV. i). Her most extensive speech to him in the play is two-and-a-half lines long – her acceptance of him again in the final scene.

Claudio is only slightly more voluble; in this whole zigzagging, on-again, off-again wooing and marriage he speaks twenty-seven lines directly to her, only two of them before the rejection scene (IV. i). Because Shakespeare chooses to develop Hero's character only sketchily she seems to be little more than a bystander at an accident. She is given little opportunity to speak out strongly in her own defence when she is insultingly cast aside for Shakespeare takes a hint from the source and has her swoon. All the arrangements for her supposed death and reappearance are conducted by her elders, Hero submitting mutely to them as she has done in previous decisions. Shakespeare accomplishes the remarkable feat of conducting all the complications of Hero and Claudio's relationship – initial wooing, acceptance, betrothal, rejection at church, repentance and renewal of marriage ceremony while allowing them to share a total of forty-one lines of direct address. Hero might well be a warning of what can happen to a woman if she doesn't shape up and become a Viola, a Rosalind or a Helena. Shakespeare chose to embellish his sources by adding the scintillating duels of wit between Beatrice and Benedick, which stand out the more effectively because of the lack of substance and the witlessness in the relationship of Hero and Claudio. The irony in the contrast is unmistakable. If the young lovers come unstuck because they have so rarely spoken we learn that verbal interaction can also be a barrier to knowledge of another. In the overhearing scenes Beatrice and Benedick are made to pause and listen; only after the cascade of scornful words that they pour on each other is turned off can they come together.

In *Troilus and Cressida* Shakespeare limits the access the audience has to a key character of the story. Spectators of a dramatization of the events of the Trojan war will expect to meet Helen, the cause of the ten-year struggle. The audience's curiosity is piqued by the Prologue which gives a detailed account of her relations to the origins of the war. Early in the play we have references by Pandarus to Helen (I. i. 39–41, 71–4), comments by Cressida on Helen (I. ii. 1–4, 48), Pandarus' gossipy account of Helen and the jest about the hair on Troilus' chin (I. ii. 88–160). The whole of the Trojan debate is devoted to the varying versions of the worth of Helen (II. ii). In the Greek camp we have Thersites' snarling contempt for a war that is caused by a whore and a cuckold (II. iii. 68–71). Yet well over 1400 lines, nearly 45 per cent of the play, pass before Shakespeare brings Helen herself on stage. Almost one-quarter of those lines are devoted to references to Helen and to her position among the Trojans as cause and continuing pretext for the war.

An audience must inevitably speculate whether she is a theme of honour and renown or a whore. No matter what clues we pick up from Pandarus' report of Helen we can never be quite prepared for the vain, frivolous creature who eventually appears. '*This* is the pearl of great price?' we gasp in astonishment. Helen, to put it mildly, does not deliver on her advanced billing. Shakespeare has set us up for what we would call today a 'non-event'. It is not so much that we mind Pandarus in III. i being made a doting fool but rather that Helen and Paris, in devoting themselves so completely to their puerile teasing, are an image of decadence for which even Thersites' bitterness has not prepared us. That so much debate and battle has been waged around this botchy core seems ludicrous. Shakespeare can make his point with extraordinary economy. Helen is on stage for less than 100 lines. She has a mere two dozen lines to speak. Her longest speech lasts four lines. Shakespeare never brings her on stage again. She is mentioned on only two more occasions in the play. When Diomed and Paris discuss her worth (IV. i. 51–79) we recognize the force and the accuracy of the Greek's ruthless evaluation of her.

Shakespeare develops different strategies of separation for the young lovers of his story. All of the on-stage interaction between Troilus and Cressida is confined to three scenes. They are together on the stage for one-tenth of the play's lines. But more important still is the fact that we only see them alone together on stage for a little more than 100 lines. Because Troilus is so inept a lover and because Pandarus bobs on and off the stage trying to expedite matters we never have even the remotest sense of the kind of lyrical, soaring ecstasy which Romeo and Juliet achieve in the balcony scene. We can tell a good deal about the way Shakespeare produces in the audience an awarenss of the superficial nature of the love of Troilus and Cressida by the amount of space he devotes to the fourth occasion when they share the stage but do not meet (V. ii). Cressida's 'private' meeting with Diomed lasts twice as long as any of the three occasions she was allowed to be alone with Troilus. In this scene of betrayal she speaks almost half as many lines to Diomed as she ever speaks to Troilus. Troilus starts his lovesick reflections on Cressida in the opening moments of the play and with a faltering, indirect, adolescent gaucheness only comes to the point of sharing her bed when the play is half over. Though Diomed declares his intention of seducing Cressida when he claims her in the Trojan camp, Shakespeare is careful to have her speak not a word to him until their secret assignation. Diomed traverses the ground Troilus had so laboured over in one swift sequence (V. ii. 5–101). Troilus is stunned by the ease with which the predatory Greek swoops down to grasp his prize.

Another strategy of separation, that of denying the audience a climactic interaction by reporting it as an off-stage event, is seen at its most effective towards the end (V. ii) of *The Winter's Tale*. The audience has been primed for a scene it has long anticipated, a witnessing of the joy of Perdita's return to Leontes, of Polixenes' forgiveness of his son, of the marriage of Florizel and Perdita – the traditional reconciliations of the last scenes of comedies and romances. But this is not the scene that we see on stage. A number of anonymous gentlemen, who have shared in the joy taking place just out of our sight, come on to give us second-hand accounts of the unravelling of the confusion and the boundless happiness which has resulted. They speak with the airy complacency of privileged insiders about which pretty touches they enjoyed most. The audience, like famished guests invited to a feast, must wait outside the door and subsist on crumbs. Several critics have noted that Shakespeare handles the scene in this way the better to focus on the reconciliation of Leontes and Hermione. Two reconciliations might be too much of a good thing. What needs emphasis is the effect of the surprise this scene gives an audience which has no knowledge that Hermione is alive. No play in the repertory had ever ended with minor, unfamiliar characters winding up the action. The only way the audience can cope with its considerable disorientation in this scene is to intuit, even before the visit to the statue is broached, that this cannot be the real ending, that there must be another last scene which is not in Greene's *Pandosto*, thus opening itself up to the possibility of a miracle. Though her death has been harped on again and again, as soon as we see the statue of Hermione unveiled we are caught up in wonder and move precisely in step with Leontes. The conviction grows in us that after experiencing one anticlimax in the report of action off stage, Shakespeare is unlikely to follow it with another one on stage – Leontes gazing on a statue that does indeed turn out to be the work of Julio Romano. An art appreciation class at this point will not quite overwhelm us with joy. The audience which misses out on the first round of reconciliations can enjoy the presentation of unexpected ones – Leontes with Hermione, Hermione with Perdita, Hermione with Polixenes – which dispel all the shadows left lingering from the first half of the play. Shakespeare acts very much like a magician who prepares for a climactic trick and bungles it to make it seem impossible only to bring off a trick even more astonishing than the one he had initially promised.

All the strategies of separation I have described so far were more fully developed by Shakespeare as central elements in the structural designs of his major tragedies. I will glance briefly at one and in closer detail at two others to indicate the ingenuity Shakespeare uses in working on an audience.

The lack of access Claudio has to Hero or Orsino to Olivia emphasize the flimsy basis of experience on which the relationships are established. Shakespeare, however, uses physical separation for a completely different effect in the relationship of Antony and Cleopatra, characters who have a very detailed knowledge of each other before we ever meet them. Plutarch's account of their lives naturally notes their frequent physical separation. But it gives only hints of the psychological effects of that separation which Shakespeare makes a central aspect of his play. The scenes devoted to Cleopatra languishing in Egypt in Antony's absence are not based on Plutarch and seem to be entirely Shakespeare's invention. The lovers and their concerns dominate almost every scene in the play, yet when we examine the structure of the play in detail we can see how severely Shakespeare has limited the stage-life they share. In the 3023 lines of the play only a little more than one-sixth is given over to those vivid sequences when they are on stage together. In his various political struggles Antony appears in eleven of the play's forty-two scenes, over 900 lines, without Cleopatra. She, pining for Antony, and calculating how to bind him, appears in five scenes, over 700 lines, where he has no part. In other words, for over half of the play's length we see them functioning in each other's absence. Between the time when Antony departs for Rome (I. iii. 105) and the moment when he reunites with Cleopatra before Actium (III. vii. 20) there are over 1200 lines, or 40 per cent of the play, 'this great gap of time', in which they make no appearance together. The play shuttles back and forth between Rome and Egypt and there are only 850 lines when one or the other of them is not on stage. So their volatile confrontations are a relatively small part of the complex relationship we come to understand. They share the stage in eleven scenes but on only three of these occasions do their interactions last for more than fifty lines. The longest single interaction they share on stage is the 110 lines when Antony explodes in furious attacks on the Cleopatra he believes is conniving with Caesar (III. xiii. 85–194). It is because the characters know each other so well that Shakespeare can make such relatively short sequences have such remarkable impact. From the opening moments of the play almost all of their meetings are stormy. Since the whole relationship is conducted more or less at boiling point Shakespeare can give us the emotionally charged sequences in which they boil over. These characters have always played elaborate games with each other as we know from one of their most vivid meetings, their first encounter on the Cydnus. There is no clearer demonstration of Shakespeare's ability to convey the nature of a relationship by indirect means. He devotes to Enobarbus' hypnotic account of the Cydnus meeting to Agrippa and Maecenas more lines than to all but two of the eleven actual meetings the audience witnesses. What Shakespeare understood from his sources was that these were lovers who could not live with each other and could not live without each other. In giving three times as much of them without each other he avoids any risk of wearying an audience with their wrangling. In this story, as in others, Shakespeare expresses one of the great paradoxes of love. Our full engagement in the tragedy derives in some degree from our awareness that this love which has so few and such brief occasions to express itself is so often given over to bitter recriminations. Early in the play Antony expresses his reaction to the very pressures Shakespeare formulates for his relationship to Cleopatra:

> Now for the love of Love and her soft hours,
> Let's not confound the time with conference harsh.
> There's not a minute of our lives should stretch
> Without some pleasure now.

(I. i. 44–7)

The moments of harmony in this play are sublimely moving and to a large extent that is because they are so hard won and so rare.

In *Macbeth* we find Shakespeare consistently separating off his two leading characters from those around them and then from each other. The ineluctable drift into isolation from the human community is emphasized visually from the outset in scene after scene. In his first encounter with the Weird Sisters (I. iii) Macbeth steps aside in soliloquy, then speaks to Banquo and then separates himself from Banquo, Ross and Angus to pursue his thoughts – 'Look how our partner's rapt.' The proportions are established. In a scene of 156 lines he directs only ten to Banquo, ten to the Weird Sisters, and speaks twenty lines in soliloquy. This pattern of moving aside from interaction with others is very common in the play. When he is welcomed on his return from battle by Duncan (I. iv), Macbeth again steps aside to speculate. Only when he arrives home will he have someone with whom he can share his 'horrible imaginings', but even there his tormented conscience leads him almost immediately into distressed solitary musings. In Holinshed, a main source for the play, Lady Macbeth has no prominent role. There are various other possible sources from which hints for her character may have been taken, but the development of the Macbeths as secret partners in crime seems to be largely Shakespeare's invention. He brings them together in sinister complicity in the murder of Duncan only to initiate a process of psychological alienation between them immediately. On his return from the murder Macbeth is scarcely capable of attending to his wife's urgent demands that he undertake the necessary precautions to conceal his act. His speeches are rather less than direct communication with his wife (II. ii. 18–41). His mind is still back in Duncan's chamber where heaven made one last appeal through the innocent, sleeping grooms and he turned down the primrose path which ensures his exile from the human community. Hints for the image of a tyrant isolated in his castle exist in the sources, but it took Shakespeare's ingenuity to find such a variety of ways to exhibit a man wearily lost in his own crimes drifting out of contact with everyone around him. We can gain some sense of this process of separation if we note that some 260 lines, over a tenth of the play, are devoted to soliloquies and asides and all but thirty of these lines are given to Macbeth and his wife. In the banquet scene (III. iv) Macbeth steps aside to talk with Banquo's murderers. He is so stricken with horror upon the arrival of Banquo's ghost that he seems unaware of the presence of others. This separation in the most public, formal scene of the play makes the point in the strongest visual terms that Macbeth is now isolated from his peers. When the ghost disappears he makes a brief recovery only to recoil more violently on the second visitation. The fact that he is alone in perceiving the ghost seems to be a signal that he is not only exiled from his court but also from any continuation of shared experience with his wife.

This technique of isolating a Machiavellian villain is common in other plays of the period but nowhere is it pursued with the rigour and inventiveness applied by Shakespeare here. He imposes very severe limitations on Macbeth's dramatic interactions. Of the major characters, besides Lady Macbeth and the Weird Sisters, he speaks extensively only to Banquo, though even to him he speaks less than forty lines, and that relationship is terminated halfway through the play. He scarcely ever speaks to his chief political opponents. In the entire play he is on stage for less than ninety lines with Malcolm and speaks only two lines directly to him. To Macduff he speaks less than forty lines, only fourteen of them before he meets him in combat at the end of the play. Indeed by the end of the banquet scene the Macbeths have drifted so far away from the bond of human fellowship that we might well wonder how Shakespeare is going to develop any significant interactions for the rest of the play.

There are 919 lines remaining in the play and virtually no one left to talk to, and in fact Shakespeare never has Macbeth and his wife interacting in the same scenic frame for the rest of the play. The only significant characters left to whom Macbeth might talk are the Weird Sisters, and his visit to them (IV. i) further emphasizes his isolation. After that visit he makes no appearance on stage for four scenes and 433 lines. Until he confronts Macduff in a combat to the death he speaks to no major character. Of the 919 lines after the banquet scene Macbeth appears on stage for only 268 of them. He is a man who has created a vacuum around himself, a man left with only servants to tyrannize over, reduced to talking only to such as Seyton, the doctor, Young Siward or a cream-faced loon, and obsessively in his disillusion, within his empty castle, to himself. This isolation is highlighted the more by contrast in the scene between Malcolm and Macduff in England. The play to that point is focused almost entirely on the career of Macbeth with very little time devoted to characters who might consider acting for the general good. By pretending to embody corruption and then casting it aside Malcolm seems to exorcize it from the play and signals a turn in the tide of events. In the expressions of sympathy for the slaughter of Macduff's family Shakespeare allows himself plenty of space to re-establish fellow-feeling and decency in a play which has dispensed with them for so long. Shakespeare has given us no insight into Malcolm and little more than a sketch of Macduff, the characters who are to root out tyranny.

The close alliance forged between Malcolm and Macduff could be given no greater contrast than the scene which follows it – the guilt-stricken Lady Macbeth sleepwalking, now with only herself to talk to, in complete isolation from her husband. The strategy of separation which so rigorously circumscribes her interactions is carried to an extreme which Shakespeare rarely matches elsewhere. She speaks a few lines of welcome to Duncan (I. vi). Upon the discovery of his murder she speaks twice briefly before fainting. In the banquet scene she speaks three times in attempts to calm the lords startled by her husband's behaviour. In the 540 lines she is on stage she is with Macbeth alone, in soliloquy, or in the total isolation of her haunted sleepwalking for over 300 of them. She has about 240 lines to speak but she directs to characters other than Macbeth only about thirty of her lines. In terms of symmetry she is placed very carefully in the play. There are 292 lines to the point where she first enters reading Macbeth's letter. There are 291 lines left in the play after her last exit in the sleepwalking scene (V. i). We have a sense of Macbeth contemplating his career before his wife spurs him on and completing his career after she has fallen by the wayside. When we first meet her she is alone and eagerly determined to be an instrument of disorder as she contemplates the murder of Duncan. When we last see her she is lost in her own mind, an image of the disorder she has helped to unleash, just as Macbeth, presented at the outset as a great warrior winning honours, is at the end a lone warrior losing in battle all the honours he has won. Macbeth is so overwhelmed by bad news that he can display no more than exhaustion on hearing of his wife's death. He is given no counsellors to turn to and, though he is intending to fight a battle, Seyton is the only figure available to receive instructions. Macbeth is, as he says himself, a bear tied to the stake who must fight alone against an army baying for his blood. Malcolm notes, 'Both more and less have given him the revolt/ And none serve with him but constrained things/Whose hearts are absent too' (V. iv. 12–14). The dark, bleak atmosphere of the play stems not only from the poetry but from the tight limitation of interactions imposed on the two major characters. Nowhere else does Shakespeare undertake this feat of locking two major characters almost entirely into their own personal hells. On the face of it it would seem impossible to dramatize a story by refusing to bring into play any extended interaction between three-quarters of the characters who constitute the personae of the play. It is another example of Shakespeare's ability to choose less and make it more.

In *King Lear* the separation which Shakespeare maintains for so long between the King and his youngest daughter is a key element which he adopted from the source play. But the way he chooses to handle the role of Cordelia and strictly deny the audience direct access to her for so long is significant. The long absence which Shakespeare maintains by sending Cordelia off in the first scene and keeping her off stage until late in the play has no parallel in the chronicle-play source. When Shakespeare decided to combine a story about Gloucester and his sons with the Lear plot he had to cut some things from the original story to make place for his new material. It is instructive to note what he cut out, what he expanded, and what additions to the main plot he invented. He develops for Lear a central relationship with a Fool. He exhibits in heartbreaking detail the processes of mental instability which afflict Lear and he achieves a special poignancy in the development of the King's relationship with Poor Tom. He also adds considerable complexity to the role Kent fulfils as loyal counsellor. He does not cut down the roles of the corrupt daughters, rather he expands them by involving them in competition for Edmund. But what Shakespeare most obviously dispenses with in *The True Chronicle Historie of King Leir* are the scenes which give

Cordella a much more continuing stage-life – in her own plans for marriage, in preparing to aid her father, in engaging in battle for him, and in restoring him to the throne – so that she is clearly the second most salient character in the old play.

We can get some idea of the change in the proportions of the story if we note how Shakespeare cuts down on the cumbersome opening of the earlier play. *Leir* devotes seven scenes and 742 lines, almost a third of the play, to the rejection of Cordella, the marriages of Gonorill and Ragan, the division of the kingdom, the wooing and winning of Cordelia by the French King and the rejection of Perillus, Kent's prototype. Shakespeare manages to telescope all of this material into 306 lines of the first scene which takes up rather less than one-tenth of his play's length, and he manages also to introduce Gloucester and Edmund, as well as Burgundy, as competitors for Cordelia's hand. Shakespeare deliberately sacrifices the focus of attention given to the relationship of France and Cordelia which establishes them, in the chronicle-play, as important allies throughout Leir's troubles and which convinces us, despite all of his vicissitudes, that a happy ending is probable. After the reconciliation of father and daughter the movement towards a restoration of Leir as head of his realm is never in doubt. In the old play's thirty-two scenes Cordella appears on stage at regular intervals in eight of them. She is on stage for a third of the play's lines and she speaks almost a tenth of those lines. By contrast in Shakespeare's play Cordelia appears in five of the twenty-six scenes, speaks in four, and shares the stage with Lear in three. After the opening there are sixteen scenes, almost two-thirds of the play, before she makes another appearance. She is on stage alive for 378 of the play's 3195 lines, less than an eighth of the play, and she speaks about 110 lines, less than one-thirtieth of the play. In other words the old play gives her three times more prominence in her on-stage life than Shakespeare gave to her. As a point of comparison that mere shuttlecock Oswald is on stage in twice as many scenes for a total of considerably more lines, and speaks almost as many lines as Cordelia does. That is not to say that she is less significant than her prototype, Cordella. For his ultimate purposes Shakespeare extracts as much significance as he can from her very absence.

The most moving moment in the play, conceivably in world drama, is the reconciliation scene between Lear and his daughter. It is instructive to note how carefully Shakespeare prepares us for that moment by references to Cordelia and news of her which keep our hopes of her re-entry into the action shadowily alive. Soon after she has left court Lear begins to worry that he has made a mistake in his treatment of her (I. iv).

Kent in the stocks (II. ii) tells us that he is in contact with Cordelia, and later (III. i) sends a message to her on her arrival with French forces in England. Edmund implicates his father in a conspiracy with the French invaders (III. v). In the following scene (III. vi) the action is initiated to take Lear to Dover where Cordelia is encamped. Cornwall makes his response to the French invasion (III. vii) and blinds Gloucester for the part he has played in helping Lear to escape. We hear of Goneril's preparation for battle against the French (IV. ii). We are told that France has returned to his kingdom leaving Cordelia to conduct his forces (IV. iii). So we are not allowed to forget that Cordelia is coming to Lear's and England's aid, but whereas the old playwright presented on stage four scenes in the French camp Shakespeare reduces all news of her to report.

At any point after we learn that Cordelia is in England (III. i) it would have been possible to present her on stage receiving news of her father. Though Lear is set in motion towards Cordelia in III. vi, Shakespeare then interposes seven scenes, over 700 lines, before they finally come into each other's presence on stage. All of these scenes which focus on the weakness of Albany, the savagery of Cornwall, the wanderings of blind Gloucester, the mad analyses of Lear, contribute to our sense of the ascendancy of the new tyrannical rulers. In report Cordelia's sympathy gives us hope of a counter-movement, but Shakespeare intuited that her physical presence on stage would be too strong. What we are being moved to accept is that Lear has caused a breach in nature that is too great to be bridged. This strategy is developed to prepare for the fundamental change Shakespeare chose to make in the ending of the story, for his play is not to conclude with the happy reconciliation of father and daughter. In Kent's report of how Cordelia took the news of her father's treatment by his dog-hearted daughters we learn that Lear, now in the town of Dover close to Cordelia in the French camp, 'by no means/Will yield to see his daughter' (IV. iii, 40–1). When Cordelia does finally return to the stage after her long absence (IV. iv) we are told that Lear has escaped and is running madly about the fields. Cordelia ends the scene hoping 'Soon may I see and hear him'. But Shakespeare postpones the reconciliation even longer to give us the scene with the blind Gloucester and Edgar meeting Lear, the scene that is the fullest expression of Lear's philosophy of the savage and chaotic handy-dandy world.

It is not only the simplicity of the language which makes the reconciliation scene (IV. vii) so powerful. It is its brevity. In the old chronicle work the reconciliation scene is a fulsomely extended affair. It is marred by an excess of humble kneeling; Cordella kneels twice, Leir twice, the King of France and one of his lords kneel, so that it comes close to a kind of parlour game. As the climax of the play it is, at 263 lines, the longest scene in the play and twice as long as most of the others. Shakespeare keeps us waiting for his reconciliation scene almost from the moment Cordelia leaves England, yet after such a long wait we are given a mere forty-two lines. Lear awakes at IV. vii. 42 and goes off with Cordelia at IV. vii. 84. They are some of the most heartrending lines ever written but the brevity is the more effective in view of the fact that Lear and Cordelia are very soon to be presented in defeat as prisoners. Every audience is shocked by this reversal in their fortunes, but it has been induced to accept this inevitability because Shakespeare, altering the proportions of the old play, has shown us so much of the evil forces at work and so very little of the counter-movement. And from the point where Lear wakes to meet his daughter again Shakespeare allows Cordelia only six lines of direct speech to him.

After Lear's defeat Shakespeare focuses on a dual movement, the attempt of Lear to maintain his relationship with Cordelia and the triumph of the good forces too late to ensure the continuation of the one relationship that has meaning for the King. The scenes and interactions which Shakespeare chooses *not* to dramatize are instructive. Lear never shares the stage with Goneril and Regan again, save with their corpses at the end, after he storms out on them at Gloucester's castle at the end of Act II. Though he is involved in battle with them he never meets them. Only Edmund has dealings with him as a prisoner. After all the torments he has suffered at their hands one might expect some scene in which he harangues them in final reckoning. But such a scene would have returned us to the bitter quarrelling of the first two acts and the mood Shakespeare is building around the isolation of Lear and Cordelia would have been dissipated. The changed and humbled Lear has no interest in his other daughters; when told of their deaths at the end he barely registers the facts. Indeed from the reconciliation scene to Cordelia's death Lear speaks almost entirely to her and scarcely acknowledges the presence of any of the other characters crowding the stage. When they are haled off to prison Lear, unlike Cordelia, speaks not a word to Edmund. He concentrates entirely on the joy that confinement with his newly recovered daughter will bring to him. Though Lear on the heath has been involved with Poor Tom, Kent, the Fool and Gloucester, at the end two of them are kept off stage and their deaths are reported, Edgar is never addressed by Lear, and Kent gets only distracted remarks from his heartbroken master. Lear's fury at the loss of Cordelia is underscored by the impossibility of his realizing a renewed or continuing relationship with anyone else on stage. With the dead Cordelia in his arms he accuses them as murderers and traitors all, but turns ever back to her. Following this most harrowing moment Shakespeare knew that there was another sequence that he could not dramatize. In other tragedies we are allowed to turn away from chaos to anticipate the future in the re-establishment of order which designates a new ruler. By priming our anticipation of the reconciliation of Lear and Cordelia, by holding it off for so long, by making it so brief and by then allowing the relationship to become the 'great thing of us forgot', he has brought us to a situation where nothing further can be said. By the method he chooses in handling the separation of Lear and Cordelia he separates the audience from any sense of meaningful continuity. Clichés, platitudes, the habitual method of reducing catastrophe to manageable proportions will not do. If we are able to say anything at all it will have to be 'what we feel, not what we ought to say'.

Shakespeare started his career writing of a king, Henry VI, progressively cut off in isolation from his realm. He ended his career with the magician, Prospero, healing the wounds that have separated him from his realm. It is in *The Tempest* that Shakespeare finally had the audacity to show us how much the art of drama depends on the manipulation of characters – keeping them apart, sending them on wild goose chases, provoking them to treachery which misfires, drawing them all together into one unified conception of humanity that does not exclude an airy sprite or a witch's child. The action of the play presents Prospero's absolute control over a dozen other characters. A good deal of Shakespeare's success depends on his ability to make a virtue of necessity. The seeming limitations of his stage, the size of his acting company, the sprawling stories he often chose to dramatize draw from him ingenious solutions. But like all of the very greatest dramatists he finds insufficient challenge in those workaday problems and, therefore, devises for himself seemingly insurmountable obstacles for the pleasure of triumphing over them. He sets himself, in *The Tempest*, a seemingly impossible challenge – the organization of a story in which he denies to his main character all but a mere handful of the possible interactions to piece out his play. The story Shakespeare devised depends on Prospero putting the visitors he has shipwrecked on his island through a variety of hoops before he reveals himself to them. The moment of revelation, which will clarify for the characters what the audience already knows, begins to accumulate power from the moment Prospero recounts his history to Miranda. He chooses to reveal himself for only the last fragment of the action (V. i. 106–318), a little over 200 lines of a play more than 2000 lines long. Until that point he exchanges speech directly with Miranda, Ferdinand and briefly with Caliban. It is the invention of Ariel as intermediary agent which allows the magician to remain apart from the action he orchestrates, and Ariel, invisible to all but his master, is denied normal verbal exchanges with all of the other characters. In other words the dramatist endows his central character with the magic of manipulation and with his own well-honed skill of achieving power by indirect means. Prospero dominates the stage in a manner that no other Shakespearian character – no king, emperor, ghost, not even Oberon who is troubled by Puck's mischief – is allowed to do. The occasional irritable signs of tyranny in his dealings with Caliban, with Ferdinand, and even with Miranda and Ariel tend to make his power a little less inhuman. But his capacity through Ariel to organize his world without stirring from his cell gives us a sense of his unchallengeable control. It is as true of art as of magic that it is the more powerful and impressive the less visible effort it seems to have taken. Shakespeare knew how to develop the artifice which conceals art, the relaxed power which makes his control over an audience invisible. For many years he had shown the varied ways in which dramatic power could be extracted from the separation of characters. Shakespeare here not only says farewell to his art, he gives us an open demonstration of how he has held sway over us. His stage has been a charmed island where characters from remote regions, distant times, and different levels of society are manoeuvred, kept apart in interwoven strands of action so that their eventual coming together may give the audience the satisfaction it has been led to anticipate for so long.

The limiting of the access characters have to each other is not a device peculiar to Shakespeare. The Greek dramatists, in presenting climactic events as off-stage action in the report of messengers, developed it as a key aspect of structure. One of the most celebrated plays in the modern theatre is worked around the singular joke of refusing twice to give any on-stage life to an eagerly awaited Godot. The split-second timing of having characters fail to meet is often the basic device which keeps comedy and farce in motion. This separation of characters is a motif which appears in the literature of many ages. We may wonder, nevertheless, how Shakespeare's use of the effects and strategies of separation developed in such an ingeniously rich variety. Separation is especially prominent as a conventional theme in the literature of courtly love. Shakespeare, in his sonnet cycle, meditates in various moods on the joys and despairs of intermittent contact with a loved one. Because the object of his regard is, for most of the cycle, a male friend, he does not have available the conventional explanation for the torments of physical remoteness – the coldly indifferent or disdainful mistress. There are geographical, physical separations about which the poet laments and suffers, but there are many more obstacles to closeness that his anxious mind forces on him – the poet's age, his rank, rivals for patronage, the mistress who attracts his patron's attention, his own projected death, the possibility of his patron's death. Seen from this angle the whole cycle revolves around the idea of exercising the mind to discover modes of contact which compensate for the absence of the loved one. Thirty-five of the sonnets are directly involved in reacting to the various effects of separation. Shakespeare takes the posture of one who is constrained to make a virtue of necessity and to find positive as well as negative results from the infrequency of direct face-to-face contact. One of the pleasures clearly is the provocation of the imagination to ingenuity, the exuberant exercise of the sonnet-writing skill itself. The other is the heightening of emotional intensity in the relationship as a result of separations. It is this idea, developed with great ingenuity in the structure of dramatic interactions, that was one of the major contributions Shakespeare, the sonneteer, made to Shakespeare, the playwright.

In comedy and tragedy, history and romance Shakespeare took every advantage possible of violating the classical unities of time, place and action to enhance our understanding of the difficulties men have in coming to terms with their situations, with others and with themselves. Shakespeare often shows characters gaining an understanding of others when they are separated from them. He knew, too, that an audience may attend to and value a relationship more if it can enjoy it only on limited occasions. Some of the tough discipline of falconry which Petruchio applied to Kate is required in the control the dramatist exerts over his audience. An audience 'full-gorged' loses interest. In Sonnet 52 Shakespeare describes the intimate connection between separation and pleasure, between lack of availability and value:

So am I as the rich whose blessèd key
Can bring him to his sweet up-lockèd treasure,
The which he will not every hour survey,
For blunting the fine point of seldom pleasure.
Therefore are feasts so solemn and so rare,
Since, seldom coming, in the long year set,
Like stones of worth they thinly placèd are,
Or captain jewels in the carcanet.
So is the time that keeps you as my chest,

Or as the wardrobe which the robe doth hide,
To make some special instant blest
By new unfolding his imprisoned pride.
　Blessèd are you whose worthiness gives scope,
　Being had, to triumph, being lacked, to hope.

The richness and the power of Shakespeare's drama comes, in part, from his careful use of that 'blessèd key'.

6 · How to shoot an arrow o'er the house to hurt your brother

Methods of indirection and separation in *Hamlet*

Shakespeare worked out many ingenious variations on the basic dramatic device of postponing or limiting interaction between major characters. He was able, by a skilful use of secondary and minor characters, to build up a tense anticipation of climactic meetings. In a few of his plays this technique is applied not simply to one plot or a sequence of events, it is the dominating factor in the organization of the whole structure of the play. The action of *Hamlet* is developed around two characters locked in a deadly struggle who hardly ever share the stage together. It has often been observed that Polonius's declaration that he will 'By indirections find directions out' (II. i. 66) applies rather more generally than merely to his own concern to spy on Laertes's extracurricular activities at university. Virtually every aspect of the plot is concerned with the use by Claudius and Hamlet of intermediaries, methods of indirection, to outfox each other. On several occasions there are accounts of scenes we have already witnessed on stage so that we can see how events are altered in recall. These reports are not concerned with events in widely separated locales. For all but four scenes of the play Hamlet and Claudius are both living in Elsinore. The frequency of reporting by shuttling interme-diaries reinforces our sense of the play as an elaborate game of hide-and-seek – a game Hamlet quite consciously plays with Rosencrantz and Guildenstern, 'Hide fox, and all after' (IV. ii. 29), and with the corpse of Polonius (IV. iii. 33–6). The willingness of characters to eavesdrop on each other gives us the sense that devious strategies are preferred to face-to-face confrontations. There is also a persistent preoccupation with the techniques of acting, with things not being what they seem. Critics have tirelessly examined the riddling nature of the language of the play. The speeches are full of oblique references: characters are always dealing with 'windlasses and assays of bias', they 'come around' to gather the wind of each other, they 'sift' each other, try to catch the drift of another, and become ever more entangled as they search through thickets of words.

This method of indirection, of filtering reports through intermediaries, is not unique to *Hamlet*. Shakespeare uses it again and again in comedy and tragedy to produce among his characters different levels of awareness about the true facts of the situation in which they are involved. The characters in *Hamlet* have a wide variety of motives but they are engaged in a common action of trying by devious means to find out what is going on so that they will know how to act. It is beside the point to interpret the play as the story of an ineffectual prince flawed by a propensity to procrastination. Hamlet exists in a world in which nobody acts and no event can occur straightforwardly. The initial impetus to the action stems from the testimony of a ghost, hardly the most substantial guarantor of unambiguous truth. Truth is so elusive that you can only sneak up on it to catch it by surprise. Only by indirect means can Hamlet discover whether revenge is being demanded by a spirit of health or goblin damned. For tactical, personal and political reasons Claudius can only work obliquely through spies to discover whether Hamlet is essentially not in madness but mad in craft. Hamlet's great problem is that in discovering the truth for himself he must reveal his knowledge to Claudius and so make it almost impossible to act upon it. At the end of the play only three men possess the secret of the causes of the struggle between the mighty opposites and Claudius never learns how his murder of his brother was discovered. Of the eight people who die in the play only two of them have any clear understanding of the circumstances that destroy them.

Hints for the basic technique of indirection exist in the extant sources. In Saxo Grammaticus the narrative relates only two incidents in which Feng and Amleth confront each other. The testing of Amleth's supposed madness is much more protracted than in Shakespeare. Shakespeare fastens on all the possible hints in the sources which enable him to develop a central figure moving into spiritual solitude. The antic disposition is not only a defensive strategy, it is also a complex aspect of Hamlet's melancholia. The proportions within the old story are radically modified in the revelation of the Prince's many layered personality; his wit, his philosophical speculations, his gracious gifts in friendship, his mercurial moods are set in deliberate conflict with the imperatives of the revenge code. The Hamlet who speaks to Horatio, the players and the gravedigger is infinitely more attractive than the Hamlet who tries to pump himself up with passionate rhetoric into a facsimile of the dreary, fustian, two-dimensional heroes who feature so frequently in revenge dramas. At least part of the effect of this strategy is the build-up in the audience of a resistance to the desire to see a final face-to-face confrontation between Claudius and Hamlet. We know that the decisive clash must come but we are half-willing accomplices in delay.

The play begins in an atmosphere of uncertainty with guards trying to identify each other. The sceptical Horatio has to be convinced of the ghost's existence. Shakespeare works on the audience, as Hamlet in his antic disposition works on Claudius, by throwing out distracting red herrings. This play is concerned with leading people up blind alleys on unprofitable detours and so in Horatio's review of the Scandinavian political situation (I. i. 79–107), which turns out to have virtually nothing to do with the Ghost's wanderings, Shakespeare makes his audience the first victim of indirection. This method of not preparing us for the truth allows us to absorb with Hamlet the full shock of the Ghost's terrible revelation of his murder.

In preparation for the first on-stage interaction between Hamlet and Claudius (I. ii) we have a careful prologue. There are forty-one lines devoted to Claudius speaking about his marriage and responding with diplomatic initiatives to the rashness of young Fortinbras. The response to the political threat is in the characteristically indirect method of the play; Danish ambassadors are sent to old Norway to urge him to restrain the hot-blooded youth. Claudius turns then to Laertes and graciously grants his eager request to be allowed to depart for Paris. The ease of this relationship, the humble submission of a subject to his lord is designed as an effective contrast to what follows. Only half way through this first sequence in which the mighty opposites share the stage does Claudius turn to his 'son'. In the silent, brooding presence of Hamlet we have gathered some of the tension already, in Claudius's delay in addressing him we sense more. Hamlet's response to the King's first remark is a riddling 'aside', and he directs only one line at Claudius before he turns away in conversation with Gertrude. The Prince's insistence that his 'customary suits of black' are not affectation, that his grief is genuine and not acted, introduces the concern with the deceptive nature of appearances which will persist in every scene until Hamlet discovers that what seems to be friendly sword-play is a three-tiered murder plot. Claudius takes his opportunity to deliver a long lecture on what he considers to be Hamlet's unnatural persistence in grief (I. ii. 87–117). This speech, the longest Claudius delivers to Hamlet, contains more than half of the lines he speaks to him in the entire play. Despite the length of this earnest appeal Hamlet makes no response. It is Gertrude's plea that he stay in Denmark to which he assents. Hamlet shares the stage here with

Claudius for 128 lines and yet contrives to speak only one line to him. It is also a part of the strategy of the scene to have Hamlet and Laertes the subjects of the attention of the man who will cause their deaths. They both wish to leave for university but only one departs. The one whose father has died remains. They have nothing to say to each other here, but the one who departs will return, after his father's death, to wrestle in a grave and eventually to kill the one who remains.

The last part of the scene is the first of the many examples of information filtered second-hand through intermediaries. The almost seventy lines Shakespeare devotes to Hamlet's cross-examination of Horatio and the soldiers about the visitation of the Ghost which we witnessed in the previous scene would seem to be a waste. We could cut this report and maintain the first scene, or cut the first scene and witness the report, or cut both and move to Hamlet's meeting with the Ghost and lose little narrative information. But what we would lose by cutting is the dramatic method of riddling obliquely towards mysteries through thickets of reports and speculation. The Ghost does not work initially on Hamlet directly – it works on him through Horatio and the soldiers. The aim of the Ghost's mission is Claudius, but it works on him through Hamlet.

The discussions in Polonius's family embroider the theme of deceiving surfaces. Polonius follows Laertes in warning Ophelia not to take the Prince's attentions as 'tenders for true pay/which are not sterling' (I. iii. 106–7). He implies that Hamlet's declarations of love are simply a technique of indirection, 'springes to catch woodcocks':

> Do not believe his vows, for they are brokers,
> Not of that dye which their investments show,
> But mere implorators of unholy suits,
> Breathing like sanctified and pious bawds,
> The better to beguile.
>
> (I. iii. 127–31)

This describes precisely the kind of beguiling love Hamlet will meet in Claudius, Gertrude, Rosencrantz, Guildenstern, Laertes, Ophelia and Polonius himself, none of whose tenders of affection are exactly sterling.

It is appropriate that all the impetus for the action comes from a murder which was not a face-to-face confrontation. Old Hamlet was deviously killed while he was asleep. Hamlet's confrontation with the Ghost is very much an overwhelming face-to-face meeting, one of the few occasions it might seem when the truth comes directly and without any deception. The Ghost, however, in its 'questionable shape', is at the very heart of the devious riddling. Hamlet will not resolve the question until the end of the play-scene as to whether the Ghost is luring him, in a supernatural scheme of indirection, to damn his soul to hell. After the Ghost departs there is an extended illustration of Hamlet *not* reporting his experiences, a dry-run of his method of indirection. He fends off his friends, as he will shortly have to fend off all his enemies, with wild and whirling words. In the cellarage scene Hamlet with the aid of the 'old mole' herds his bewildered friends around the stage in a striking, visual image of the devious agencies at work in the play.

Polonius's instructions to Reynaldo, in elaborately periphrastic speeches, on how to spy on Laertes so his 'bait of falsehood takes this carp of truth' (II. i. 63) are a political primer on the indirect strategies employed in almost every scene of the play. Polonius swallows a bait of falsehood immediately on Ophelia's report of Hamlet's visit to her in 'the very ecstasy of love'. It is clear on many occasions how much Hamlet dislikes 'seeming' and play-acting, but in self-protection he must become the best actor of all. We suspect, however, that his performance as anguished lover for Ophelia may reflect some genuine pain as well as serving to lead his hunters, in search of explanations for his melancholy, up a blind alley. Hamlet gets the communication chain right. The story goes to Claudius through Polonius in his patented method of going from point A to point B by a circular tour conducted through points C to Z. In everything that happens there must be middle ground, middle agent, a way of coming round to instead of going straight at things. The way of cooling down Fortinbras is to curb him through old Norway. In the terms of the agreement Fortinbras is to come through Denmark to get to Poland.

The growing complications of indirect strategies are evident when Hamlet meets his newly arrived university friends. He prevents them from confessing their disloyalty to him and insists on telling them why they have been set on as spies so that they may continue to serve the King. The spies, it is evident, are of much more use to Hamlet than they are to Claudius because through them he can encourage all the false speculative theories about his madness while he finds some way of testing the Ghost's honesty. Claudius serves agents like so many tennis balls and Hamlet sends them spinning back determined to keep them in play until it is time to bat them out of court.

The report Rosencrantz and Guildenstern make to the King of their interview with Hamlet may, from the point of view of dramatic economy, seem superfluous. Rosencrantz asserts that Hamlet was 'Niggard of question, but of our demands/Most free in his reply' (III. i. 13–14), which is not quite accurate since they asked him three questions while Hamlet plied them with over two dozen and revealed to them no information that Claudius did not already possess – the more intermediaries the more filters to the truth. Spies have a vested interest in pushing their own theories. Claudius soon has too many explanations of why the Prince is lunatic. He proceeds to test the most salient theory by working through Ophelia in the first in the series of eavesdropping scenes.

Between the time when we first hear of the relationship of Hamlet and Ophelia (I. iii. 5) and the moment when, after various discussions of it due to the Prince's spectral visitation to her closet, Shakespeare brings them together on stage before the audience for the first time (III. i. 89), over 1200 lines, or almost one-third of the play, are performed. Ophelia becomes for Hamlet, in the nunnery scene, another example of the world of 'seeming' in which actors, like painted whores, lack the sincerity of direct, spontaneous feelings. Whenever Hamlet for a moment thinks he can drop his mask and open his heart he discovers that he is on stage with another spy in an undeclared play within a play. This is only the second occasion that Hamlet and Claudius share the stage but the separation is maintained between them by the arras. Hamlet puts on a bravura performance as a ranting actor. He is using the antic disposition and yet is on the borders of despair, is both lashing Ophelia for her betrayal but wishing also she were safely out of harm's way, is speaking directly to Ophelia and sending a message through her to Claudius. The message gets through more effectively than Hamlet might wish. Despite his need to keep his secret, the longer his revenge is delayed the more Hamlet feels impelled to issue oblique threats to Claudius.

The Prince's ideas on acting are not simply a matter of taste, they are critically related to his situation. To survive the spies Claudius rains on him he has to be acute in detecting a bad performance. He counsels the actors against mouthing, sawing the air, tearing a passion to tatters. It is a central paradox of this play that Hamlet depends not, as Claudius has, on real people acting, but on actors behaving convincingly like real people. Claudius's indirect assaults are transparent to Hamlet. The King's agents are all destroyed because, though they know very little of what is really going on, they are conscious of their deception in trying to discover what is wrong with Hamlet. In trying to maintain their innocence they give themselves away. Hamlet in his indirect assault uses only the actors who have no knowledge of the hidden significance of their actions and who can travel in and out of the danger zone. It is remarkable that Horatio, Hamlet's only ally, is asked to perform only the one minor task of observing Claudius at the play. That helps to explain why Horatio's relationship to Hamlet is such a relief to the audience. With the odds so heavily stacked against him it provides Hamlet with an outlet for his secret. The nature of their communication is, compared to everything else in the play, so open, face-to-face, warm and free – direct rather than indirect. We have little sense that the duplicity involved in playing the cat-and-mouse game radically compromises the characters of Claudius, Gertrude, Polonius, Rosencrantz and Guildenstern. It certainly destroys Ophelia and Laertes, but it is on Hamlet that it has the most complex effect in the way it seems to deny him the full exercise of so many of his qualities. When he is with Horatio we see the Prince's generous, open-hearted nature. The main evidence of the generosity is his refusal to embroil his friend deeply as an agent of indirection between the fell, incensed points. In spite of all the arrows being shot over the house Horatio is never in danger.

In the climactic play-scene the mighty opposites share the stage openly for only the second time. Since they last parted (I. ii. 128) over 1500 lines, 40 per cent of the play, have intervened. Hamlet has still spoken only one line to his uncle. The play-scene is as devious and indirect a method of sneaking up on a decisive confrontation as Hamlet has been able to imagine. It is an ingenious variation on the eavesdropping practised against him. Claudius's behind-the-arras work has yielded little harvest. Hamlet and Horatio, though in full view, are figuratively behind the arras. When the courtiers enter the Prince chats nervously with Polonius and Ophelia and speaks only an enigmatic riddle directly to Claudius. The players dominate the stage, but for 173 lines the audience's attention is riveted on Hamlet and the King. Claudius, master-manipulator of spies and expert of back-stage work, does not know that as audience of *The Murder of Gonzago* he is stage-centre. Shakespeare manages to develop the scene so that Hamlet directs only thirteen lines at Claudius and Claudius speaks only three lines to Hamlet. It is one of the most complete examples of the dramatic voltage which can be generated by holding two forces apart. After all of his elaborate preparation Hamlet is allowed to shout five words to assert the complete triumph of his trick: 'What, frighted with false fire?' (III. ii. 256). Claudius demands 'Give me some light' (III. ii. 259) even as he is shown in a blinding flash his own devious, serpentine nature. The player pouring poison becomes for Claudius a real man, himself, and, as a consequence, he becomes a player-king, a mockery king of snow shouting the curtain line which ends the play-within-a-play which he and Hamlet have been engaged in from I. ii to this point. Claudius has received many confusing reports from his secret agents. In the performance of the 'tragedians of the city' Hamlet delivers his report from his own secret source of information.

Out of indirections directions are found in the explosive confrontation of the play-scene. We might expect after all the circumambulatory plotting a sudden direct lunge to resolution, but the logic of the situation precludes that. It is an irony of the structure of the play that in the first half the spies which are sent to ensnare Hamlet are used by him to maintain his secret and his freedom. In the second half the antic disposition which has acted as protection for Hamlet is used by Claudius to maintain the secret and to pack him off to England. Because Hamlet now appears in everyone's eyes, save Horatio's, to be a dangerous lunatic threatening usurpation he has no power and could compel no belief in exposing the King's villainy. The only path left is back into the shadows of indirection. Hamlet and Claudius play out their roles now not for each other but for the public. Hamlet knows that Claudius must hope to kill him and bury his secret while his only hope is to catch the King unguarded.

In the prayer-scene (III.iii) Hamlet seems to get the chance he needs – his enemy alone. Claudius killed old Hamlet when his back was turned and his soul unprepared. Claudius, alone, unprotected, with his back turned is, ironically, in the only posture that can save him. Hamlet wants a face-to-face revenge and considers that killing Claudius with a shriven soul would hardly be just recompense for his father's wandering in purgatorial agony. Hamlet is on stage alone with several other characters for considerable periods. The only time he is on stage alone with Claudius is for these twenty-four lines where they do not speak to each other but where Hamlet muses on the precision of the revenge he requires (III. iii. 73–96). In this one speech he has half as many lines *not* directed at the King physically in his presence as on all the occasions when he does interact with him. The Prince has been taken in by none of the actors who have tried to work on him so far. But Claudius, without knowing it, does deceive him by being in the posture of a penitent. The moment after Hamlet departs Claudius reveals that he cannot achieve contact with heaven. This is the lynch-pin of the whole method of indirection. Once ensnared in such complexity the possibility of direct action becomes illusory. Revenge is postponed by something very like the 'seeming' Hamlet once defined so well: windy suspiration of forced breath, the fruitful river in the eye, dejected havior of the visage, forms, moods and shapes of grief, actions that a man might play. So the protagonists will soon separate for 800 lines and the plot moves on to the slaughter of eight people, the disastrous harvest of duplicity, because at this point one thrust of the sword is not possible. Only thirty lines later a direct thrust through the arras is possible but that turns out to be another example of indirection, Claudius's means of separating himself from Hamlet.

Claudius no longer needs the speculations and secret evidence his spies can glean, yet he must now go along with the zeal of his spies and act the ignorance he formerly experienced. Polonius is allowed to proceed on his fool's errand to the Queen's chamber but Claudius does not join him behind the arras.

Shakespeare has severely limited the Prince's interactions not only with Claudius but also with the other two major figures in his life, his mother and the ghost of his father. He renews contact with both of them in the bedroom scene (III. iv). At this point over 60 per cent of the play has been acted out and yet we have observed interaction between Hamlet and his mother only on two occasions (I. ii; III. ii) for a total of less than thirty lines. From a number of remarks, to Horatio, to the Ghost, and in his soliloquies, we know how much his grief and mental turmoil are related to his mother's remarriage. All of the cryptic and oblique hints store up a dramatic voltage which Shakespeare can release in the bedroom scene. The pent-up fury which has not found release in action against Claudius is turned into a verbal siege against Gertrude. The only advancement of the plot in the scene is the killing of Polonius and that is accomplished almost immediately. It allows us to see that Hamlet is capable, as always, of impulsive action. The Claudius he wants, the adulterate beast dressed in all his sins, eludes him twice – once in seeming prayer, once in seeming to be eavesdropping behind the arras. For an instant revenge looks simple, but it eludes him again when he uncovers the corpse of an intruding fool peripheral to the issue.

The rest of the scene dilates upon the complexity of the emotional responses that trouble Hamlet. It looks as if we have a breakthrough to plain-speaking. The Prince unpacks his heart and falls to cursing his mother like a very drab. The scene is another complex exhibition of indirection however. Because of the Ghost's injunction (I. v. 84–8) Hamlet cannot share the burden of his terrible secret with his mother. In the first attack on her it is almost as if he is trying to recover the time before catastrophe struck his family, the period when his father and Claudius were, like two pictures, available for comparison. How was it possible to move from Hyperion to a satyr, from a fair mountain to a moor? We see even more clearly how difficult it is for Hamlet to act in the present because of his inability to come to terms with the events of his past. The action of revenge is, in some ways, peripheral here to Hamlet's need to know whether Gertrude was confederate with Claudius against his father. His mind follows the track of indirection; by trying to escape into the past it circles inevitably back to the hideous reality of the present in the evocation of the vivid, inexpungeable image of the nasty sty of incestuous love. The Ghost appears at precisely the moment Hamlet reveals to himself the gorgon image which so distracts him. We are reminded of the moment when the Ghost, with his simple imperative, set Hamlet on the complex path of revenge. Because the Ghost knows exactly what happened in the past it knows what must happen in the future. Hamlet has only just achieved the certainty which the Ghost possessed at the outset. Along the way he has had to observe how Ophelia, and his friends Rosencrantz and Guildenstern, have allowed themselves to be used against him. He has had time to contemplate his mother's remarriage, and by revealing his knowledge of the murder and even now in killing Polonius he has put himself completely in Claudius's power. Such matters are motes that trouble the mind's eye. The appearance of the unappeased spirit is one of the most vivid examples of indirection in the play. Hamlet gazes on the Ghost and urges his mother to look upon it, but she only looks piteously at her son. Hamlet is caught in the crossfire of his parents' eyes, the one trying to sharpen his resolve, the other still on detours through the antic disposition incapable of seeing 'all that is'. Gertrude is no closer to the truth of what is going on than the foolish, prating knave, Polonius, ever was, a man who could only surmise as he was dying that he had been stabbed in mistake for a rat.

Before Hamlet departs for England Shakespeare gives us the only scene in the play in which he permits any extended confrontation and continuous speech between the protagonists (IV. iii). This is the first time in the play, save for the brief instant at the end of the play-scene, when they can look into each other's eyes sharing the certain knowledge of the murder that must be avenged. Shakespeare has them on stage for only some forty lines and he has ensured that instead of direct confrontation we can have only elliptical, riddling innuendo. Hamlet chooses, in revealing the whereabouts of Polonius's body, about as indirect a way of relating a simple fact as can be imagined. He needs, in his powerlessness, to take every opportunity to mock Claudius. It is the King's technique to hide things and operate behind everyone's back! How appropriate that one of his spies should be mislaid and his agents incapable of finding the body.

Hamlet cannot refuse to be sent to England nor can he demonstrate his sanity by revealing his knowledge of Claudius's crime. The antic disposition which served him so well as a shield has now become a cage which the King can use to ship him off abroad to his death. We only have to imagine how he might phrase an appeal to remain in Denmark to see how hopeless his position is: 'I have killed Polonius because I thought he was the King in hiding. I have to kill my uncle because I met my father's ghost a few months back and he revealed to me that Claudius murdered him by pouring poison in his ear. I guarded myself from Claudius's suspicions by pretending madness until I could test whether the ghost was honest or not. Claudius gave himself away at the play. I have just met the ghost again in my mother's bedroom and he urges me to kill the King at once which I will not be able to do if you send me to England.' Would a court filled with Claudius's tools believe any of this or would they send for a straitjacket? The theatre audience would not be able to believe any of it if it had not been present at the Ghost's revelation. The evidence, to put it mildly, is circumstantial.

In Hamlet's absence we concentrate on the fatal consequences for Polonius's children in becoming tools for Claudius. When Laertes breaks open the door it looks as if we shall have at last some face-to-face dealing. He enters like a tidal wave with exactly the words Hamlet might have used: 'O thou vile king,/Gave me my father' (IV. v. 115–16). He goes on to assert 'I'll not be juggled with' (IV. v. 130) – a brave statement and easier said than done in this court of juggling. He insists he will dare damnation, something at which Hamlet baulked. Claudius assures Laertes that he has had no 'direct' or collateral hand in the death of Polonius and redirects his fury at Hamlet. In working over Laertes Claudius moves steadily to the point but throws out ingenious meanders to drive his anger on. He nudges, challenges, manoeuvres until a devious ambush is created out of an innocent sword-fight. Laertes enters like a hawk stooping to the kill and ends perched tamely on Claudius's wrist, hooded and firmly tied by the jesses of a sinister plot. In this scene alone Claudius speaks twice as many lines to Laertes as he speaks to Hamlet in the entire play. He succeeds in suborning one revenger to protect himself from the other.

On his return in the graveyard scene Hamlet gives us an account of the unusual instrumentality to which a man can indirectly descend – mighty Caesar patching a hole in a wall. In this play people are put to all kinds of uses and most of them become dust before it ends. They have as little understanding of the ends shaped for them as Alexander had in coming to stop a beer barrel. Again Shakespeare has Hamlet and Claudius briefly on stage together at the funeral of Ophelia but they exchange no words.

In his report to Horatio (V. ii) we learn how Hamlet has redirected Rosencrantz and Guildenstern as substitutes for his own execution thus ensuring for them a devious way of death for their devious betrayal. The wager on the fencing match comes through the gilded performance of Osric, the only tool used by Claudius against Hamlet to survive. His rhetorical arabesques are another way of avoiding coming directly to the point. Hamlet works wittily at separating the substance of the wager from its gaudy packaging. Shakespeare's apportioning of Hamlet's interactions with agents and incidental characters helps to highlight the severe limitation imposed on the face-to-face relationship with Claudius. He speaks four times more lines to Rosencrantz and Guildenstern than to their employer. He has twice as many lines to speak to the players, he sustains a longer conversation with the gravedigger, and speaks here as many lines to Osric in five minutes as he ever speaks to Claudius.

All of Hamlet's apology to Laertes before the fencing match is phrased in terms which suggest that all harm or insult was indirect and unintended: 'I have shot my arrow o'er the house/And hurt my brother' (V. ii. 232–3). There are some more arrows to be shot over the house before the play is done. Laertes, thinking to revenge his father and sister, is caught 'as a woodcock to mine own springe' by the poisoned, unbated foil. The poison in the chalice which Claudius has prepared to keep secret the crime which has won him the crown and the Queen is drunk by her and forced down his own throat. When Hamlet and Claudius confront each other in the final scene they are sharing the stage consciously in each other's presence for only the fifth time. Claudius is acting indirectly through Laertes as Hamlet, in the earlier climactic scene acted through the players. The issue between them is one which cannot be resolved by words. They exchange here slightly more than a dozen lines of speech. It is worth remembering that Hamlet with over 1400 lines is the longest part Shakespeare ever wrote and that Claudius speaks over 500 lines. The two characters between them speak over half the lines of the play. But in direct exchange with each other they share less than 100 lines of speech, about a fortieth of the play. Hamlet can scarcely bring himself to speak to Claudius even before the visitation of the Ghost. But on almost every occasion we see him he is talking to himself and to others about Claudius, or through others to Claudius. The only exceptions to this are the discussions with the players, with the gravedigger, and some of his remarks to Horatio. Claudius spends the whole play talking to the agents he uses to try to unmask Hamlet and to get rid of him. His attention is elsewhere only in his brief dealings with the ambassadors to Norway (I. ii; II. ii), in his observations of the mad Ophelia (IV. v), and at the play-scene where Hamlet so successfully unmasks him (III. ii). When Hamlet takes the poisoned foil which has been effectively designed for a secret, underhand murder and uses it, with a crowning irony, on the man who fully knows its deadly potency, only then does the plotting finally come out of the shadows. Hamlet has carried an enormous secret burden throughout the play. Now at last he makes a public accusation. Only in the last words that Claudius hears on earth is there a direct and open statement of the secret which has locked him in a death-struggle with Hamlet: 'Here, thou incestuous, murd'rous, damned Dane,/Drink off this potion' (V. ii. 314–15). When he delivers these words Hamlet has still spoken less than forty lines to Claudius. His statement is hardly elaborate enough to clarify anything for the amazed onlookers.

Only one of the eight deaths in the play results from an original premeditated plan, rather than from a mistake, the backfiring of the plot, or the hoisting of an engineer with his own petard. That death is Hamlet's. The ending is a *pièce de resistance* of indirection in a play obsessed with it. If Hamlet does not sweep to his revenge as he initially promises he is not alone in pursuing a zig-zagging course through the confusions of the world. He is responsible for five deaths in the play which makes him something more than John-a-dreams. By remarkably devious means it turns out that Fortinbras's revenge has been accomplished. He returns from Poland, having had no part in the action, to stumble accidentally into his profit. There remains to meet Fortinbras one man, uninjured by speculatively launched arrows, who knows why the stage is strewn with corpses. The world cannot learn the story from Hamlet's mouth but, in the manner of the whole play, must hear it by indirect report from Horatio, the man least involved in the action. Horatio's role offers one of the more remarkable and consistent examples of Shakespeare's technique of character separation. Save for the sentinels in the opening scenes, a gentleman and a sailor Horatio has speech only for Hamlet. Even when he is on stage for long periods with the gravedigger and with Osric all of his words are directed to his friend. At the end, however, he is capable of explaining not only Hamlet's death but of revealing what events have led to the deaths of Claudius, Gertrude, Polonius, Laertes, Ophelia, Rosencrantz and Guildenstern. At some point he has shared the stage with all of them and yet, in the whole play, has not spoken directly to any of them. He can reveal also how all of these deaths are connected to a murderous plot, hitherto unknown, which killed the King whose funeral originally brought him to this country.

7 · 'And what's he then that says I play the villain'

Iago, the strategist of separation

In tragedy the audience is often given knowledge that is denied to the characters. Because the audience is not subject to clouded judgment by participation in the action, it has the freedom to understand why catastrophe must occur and must watch helplessly while the characters use their freedom and proceed in ignorance to make assurance of death double sure. This burden of special knowledge with which the playwright invests his audience can be exploited in a great variety of ways. The tension experienced by the audience can be tuned to an almost unbearable level when the audience feels that the characters are ensnared in a trick of plot which simple information could dispel. Many of Shakespeare's tragedies, however, do not aim to produce a sense of helpless frustration in the audience at its inability to interfere in the course of events.

In *King Lear* we watch Lear stumbling helplessly towards madness but because he has spent a lifetime wreathed in his own illusions about the nature of his power the audience does not feel that it has any special knowledge which would help him out. Most of the things we might think of saying are being spoken to him by the Fool. As an audience we are likely rather to hang back as Lear, in his harrowing quest, constructs an arctic philosophy of the world and endeavours to impose his mad vision on everyone. Only in the writ issued for Cordelia's death are we teased by our helplessness to interfere in events, our inability to prevent the extinction of that last spark of hope in a darkening world. We do not feel inclined, in watching *Macbeth*, to call out a warning to the hero that the Weird Sisters are paltering with him in a double sense. Macbeth is not the ignorant, helpless victim of external forces. We move step by step with him into his dark knowledge of the equivocal nature of evil actions as he finds that the pursuit of power and the endeavour to maintain it empties the world of all meaning and comfort. In *Hamlet* we are not made privy to special information which could help the hero. It is true that Hamlet walks unaware into the triple treachery of the fencing match but he has, by that time, reached a level of stoical acceptance of his fate which the audience has been induced to share. We know that revenge cannot be accomplished save at the cost of his life. I am not suggesting that the audience *can* interfere in the action of the play, only that under certain circumstances the playwright can make the audience fervently wish that it could. When we spend much of our time thinking 'if only they knew', itching to pass on the simple information which would save their lives, then the playwright achieves his success by bringing the danger his characters are in tantalizingly close and yet manipulating the necessary separation which must be maintained between the audience and the drama.

In *Othello* Shakespeare made radical alterations in his source-story to produce an experience of almost unbearable tension which has no parallel in world drama. There is a convention in English pantomime which generously provides the audience with a release denied by Shakespeare in *Othello*. Early on in a pantomine the hero usually talks to the audience warning of the dangers he anticipates from the villains. He asks for the audience's help in looking out for traps that are set for him in his absence and gives a password which must be shouted out to warn him of trouble. The audience thereafter screams out the word whenever the hero is about to stumble into unexpected snares. By feigning temporary deafness the hero can tune up the audience's involvement to a delirium of lusty bellowing in a co-operative triumph over evil. *Othello* achieves its effect by reversing this process so that the audience is relentlessly victimized.

The structure of *Othello* develops in a series of improvised, undeclared playlets in which Iago organizes roles for his victims. The degree of control he maintains over the characters allows him to induce a psychological alienation and separation between some of them. This produces a physical separation which is registered by the finely judged proportions in the character interactions. Iago is helped over all the weak points in his plot by his victims themselves. Even the mere random contingency of events for a while allows all the accidents to knit up the design where it could unravel and expose Iago's villainy. We may smile indulgently at the many recorded instances of unsophisticated audiences shouting out warnings to Othello about the handkerchief, or invading the stage to belabour the unbearable villain Iago. We have to acknowledge, however, that the play's success depends on arousing our impulsive wish to stop the action and that the more, as civilized playgoers, we stifle that impulse the more the play achieves its ascendancy over us. It is not simply that we lack the release valve provided in pantomime but rather that we are confronted again and again by our helplessness We have no access to a hero who needs our help, rather we have access to the villain sharing his plans and explaining to us why the characters must fall into the roles he has shaped for them.

What makes Iago unbearable is his ability to combine two roles very familiar to an Elizabethan audience. He is very much like the intermediary, commentator friends, those blunt, honest figures who try to make the tragic heroes see the true nature of their situations – Enobarbus, Kent, Lear's Fool, Menenius Agrippa, Apemantus, Mercutio. He is a soldier, a rough diamond who is foul-mouthed, cynical, and has a low opinion of women. Because he admits to his limitations he is trusted. The role of blunt soldier and honest friend conceals a descendant of the Vice-figure, a man who is an amoral rag-bag of confused motivations invested with a cynicism so profound that he must pervert or destroy any sign of virtue. Shakespeare wrote of other tragic heroes who reject the judgment of their blunt advisers because their very natures make them incapable of cautious restraint. They must embrace their fates even at the cost of the destruction fearfully prophesied for them. Othello, however, accepts the version of reality thrust upon him by his 'honest' friend in the belief that he is saving himself from miserable embroilment in a corrupt world. Thus in most of the tragedies it is the commentating figure who, in the limitations in his understanding, enables us to come to terms with the full complexity of the fate with which the tragic hero is coping. In *Othello* it is the hero who is separated off from the full complexity of the circumstances in the world in which he exists. The very deliberate organization of the play to produce an unbearable tension around Iago as a strategist of separation can be seen in the radical changes Shakespeare makes in the source-story. Cinthio's novella contains, on the face of it, very little promise of dramatic tension. Shakespeare made many alterations of detail especially in tightening up the time-scheme of the sequence of events, in changing the military rank of the originals of Othello and Cassio, and in developing a significant political framework in which his Moor could be featured. He invents a romantic courtship between Othello and Desdemona and the objections of Brabantio to his daughter's secret alliance. He does not make any radical changes in the characters on which Desdemona and Cassio are based. Shakespeare's most significant changes in developing his scenic structures are in the dramatic methods he finds of unfolding Iago's dominating agency in the story.

Cinthio's ensign is quite a conventional villain and there is little indication in the narrative that he has any detailed interaction with any character other than the Moor in securing his aim. His motivation is explained quite clearly as a desire for Disdemona. He tries in devious ways to make her aware of his passion but she takes no notice. He imagines the corporal receives more of her favour than himself and his plot develops out of jealousy and his need for revenge. Shakespeare touches many times on an array of possible motives but they are only threads in the complex web of Iago's evil nature. Cinthio's purpose is to a large degree didactic and he has no interest in ambiguities which would cloud the issues. Shakespeare compels our attention by making us pursue a mystery which we cannot ultimately solve. Cinthio tells us that his ensign is a cunning villain, but his Janus-headed personality, his ability to be convincing in the role of honest, trusty friend, is exhibited only in relations with the Moor. The first specific example of his ability to take others in by role playing comes near the end of the novella in his attempted murder of the corporal. After he has cut off the corporal's leg the ensign runs away so as not to be discovered at the scene of the crime. He mingles with those who find the wounded corporal and grieves as if the injury were to his own brother. That is the only crisis in which Cinthio's ensign has to be fast on his feet in juggling roles. Out of that one example Shakespeare develops an accomplished performer who manipulates his various masks in virtually every scene of the play. In fact before we are 200 lines into the play, in the variety of personae Iago presents to Roderigo, Brabantio and Othello, his quick-change acting skills are more fully developed than in any circumstance Cinthio creates for his ensign. In the novella the ensign develops a plot which works directly on the Moor and involves scarcely any interaction with other characters. The ensign's wife knows of her husband's villainy but plays no part in his stratagems and, through fear of him, never reveals her knowledge. Disdemona has only one interaction with the ensign when he steals her handkerchief and one brief talk with the corporal. Shakespeare chose to make Iago's 'honesty' a central focus of the play. This allows him to develop scenic structures around the ensign's hair-raising, juggling act of conducting interactions with a variety of victims who turn to him for advice and who, between them, innocently perform the tragedy that his monstrous imagination improvises.

Shakespeare wastes no time in declaring Iago's dedication to the creation of illusion. He follows Othello to serve his turn upon him, 'trimmed in forms and visages of duty' (I. i. 50), and while he keeps his heart attending on himself he throws 'shows of service' on his lord (I. i.

52). As soon as he has completed his explanation of his theatrical nature to Roderigo (I. i. 61–5) he proceeds immediately to a demonstration of his skills as stage manager and prompter. Roderigo, unaware of his role as ventriloquist's dummy, is encouraged to arouse Brabantio and plague him with flies. Desdemona's father, pricked down by Iago for the role of bigoted *senex iratus*, plays his part flawlessly. Ignorant that he is in an undeclared play he does, nevertheless, correctly identify the role being played by the prompter shouting from the shadows. His assertion 'Thou art a villain' (I. i. 117) has both of its Elizabethan senses – the low-born man of ignoble ideas and the man disposed to criminal actions. Though his role is defined so early Iago ensures that his name is not attached to it. We will be within 140 lines of the end of the play before the man Iago destroys will be able to look at the friend he has trusted and see him for what he is – 'Precious villain!' (V. ii. 236).

One of Shakespeare's most important modifications of Cinthio's novella is the invention of Roderigo. Cinthio centres almost all of his narrative on the relationship of the Moor and the ensign, and the destruction of Disdemona. The corporal and the ensign's wife are quite marginal figures. When Shakespeare chose to structure his play around six major characters he had, mathematically, the opportunity to develop fifteen relationships for on-stage interaction among them. The fact that he chose not to activate five of those relationships at all and three of them in only a sketchy way helps us to understand how he went about the business of making a difficult story credible and compelling. The limitation imposed on Roderigo's interactions is a central example of Shakespeare's skill in developing an important character who is yet kept rigidly separated on stage from those in whose life he is enmeshed. He is in seven scenes of the play and on stage for almost 1000 of its lines. It is Othello's marriage he wants to help destroy, Cassio's reputation he ruins and Cassio's life he tries to take, but after speaking to Brabantio in the opening scene he utters less than a dozen words to characters other than Iago. In six of his scenes he is on stage alone with Iago for over 350 lines, which happens to be the second largest interaction, next only to that between Othello and Iago, observed by the audience in the play. For the other 600 lines Roderigo is on stage he is almost entirely mute. He never speaks one word to Desdemona the object of his desire, nor to Othello the object of his envy, and only one line to Cassio whom he is persuaded to murder. He is truly kept in the corner of Iago's jaw, first mouthed to be last swallowed. The fact that Shakespeare gives more on-stage life to the relationship between Iago and Roderigo than to that between Othello and Desdemona serves more purposes than showing how a villain can wind a pliable tool into his plot. Iago's contempt for his fellow men and the glib assertions of his cynical philosophy can be directed at Roderigo because, having so little regard for his 'snipe', he feels no need to hide his demonic nature. Cinthio devotes very little of his narrative to an exploration of the ensign's nature. In the interactions with Roderigo and in the soliloquies Iago speaks, Shakespeare allows the audience ample opportunity to try to understand the nature of his villain's power and the source of his grievances. We are allowed for almost one-sixth of the play to see Iago operating without his mask or with only the covering excuses to Roderigo for the villainy in which he ensnares him. Roderigo is, theoretically, a loophole in Iago's plot because he knows that Cassio was treacherously undone as the Moor's lieutenant. In spite of his knowledge of villainy, the disappointment of his hopes, and his threats to reveal what he knows Roderigo only speaks up on his death-bed.

In the Senate-scene the origin and nature of the relationship between Othello and Desdemona is discussed at length, yet Shakespeare radically limits the on-stage spoken interaction between them. Othello speaks to the senators, the Duke and Iago, she speaks to Brabantio and the Duke. They state their cases separately. Othello directs three lines to her and she speaks not a word to him. We hear the Moor's detailed account of their courting but we see nothing of it, and their married life in Venice is 'but an hour/Of love, of worldly matters and direction' (I. iii. 298–9). The romantic wooing has been conducted in the nine months Othello has spent in Venice. The basis of the attraction which draws Desdemona to Othello is no doubt more than what Iago will come to call bragging and fantastical lies, but their marriage is certainly not given the maturing of time and experience indicated in Cinthio's story. There they are allowed months of happily married life in Venice and the ensign and his plotting are not introduced until after the Moor and his wife are settled in Cyprus. But Iago can assure Roderigo and himself that as soon as Desdemona comes to know her new husband she will grow tired of him and that sanctimony and a frail vow will hardly be sufficient to hold them together.

The audience has a need of more explanations than are offered to Roderigo for the venomous revenge the ensign promises. Iago obliges: 'it is thought abroad that 'twixt my sheets/Has done my office. I know not if't be true;/But I, for mere suspicion in that kind,/Will do as if for surety' (I. iii. 381–4). The implication for the audience to take is that Iago is not so much acting from a motive, but rather amusing himself by looking for one. Roderigo is called a 'snipe', a game bird hunted in marshy areas. But Iago has us within his gunsights too. We are sitting ducks distracted by the decoy motivations he sends sailing our way. We are told that Othello 'will as tenderly be led by th' nose/As asses are' (I. iii. 393–6) even as we ourselves are being led by the nose. Iago has a considerable capacity for self-dramatization, He has an air of *grand guignol* as he reaches out for the trappings of Satanism to terrorize the audience and to give himself a sense of importance: 'Hell and night/Must bring this monstrous birth to the world's light' (I. iii. 397–8). Though Othello looks down for cloven feet on Iago at the end of the play he knows it is a fable. The ensign's invocation of satanic powers is another method of trailing his coat and piecing out motivations which will satisfy himself and his dupes, including us.

The tension which Shakespeare generates in this play is partly a result of the fact that the characters ensnared in nets are cut off from contact with us while Iago is not. The soliloquies remind me of the hypnotist's trick of turning to banter with the audience when he has frozen someone into an absurdly undignified posture on stage. The narrator of Thomas Mann's story *Mario and the Magician* is an average, decent, middle-class citizen who tries to understand why he feels compelled to stay at a performance in which a crippled grotesquely evil hypnotist, Cipolla, degrades his fellow human beings. It is clear that the magician gains ascendancy not only over his victims who perform his humiliating commands but also from those who passively watch them. At the climax of the show the magician humiliates Mario, a hotel waiter, by forcing him in trance to kiss him on the cheek as if he were his beloved. But when Mario wakes up he shoots the magician dead. The narrator then perceives that he was waiting for that fatal end as a liberation from the horror he had stayed to witness. We cannot, in *Othello*, escape an awareness that we are a source of Iago's power in acting as helpless listeners to his progress reports on his acts of villainy. We are compelled to wait for Emilia to wake from her trance and speak the truth though it costs her her life.

In Cinthio's narrative the Moor and Disdemona sail together over tranquil seas to Cyprus on business which has nothing to do with the danger or strife of war. Shakespeare builds tension out of a series of arrivals from the storm-wracked seas which have separated Othello and Desdemona. The protean Iago plays the role of court jester for the anxious Desdemona. Iago, like Thersites, regards the world as a kind of absurd theatrical spectacle designed to affirm his own cyncial evaluation of human nature. It is his rooted conviction that he is in a world of players. Cassio is 'most apt to play the sir' (II. i. 172–3). Women are players in housewifery who 'rise to play, and go to bed to work' (II. i.

115). His remarks merely illustrate how undetectable he is as a villain to Desdemona, Cassio and Emilia when he plays blunt, honest soldier. The proportions within the scene are typical of the general design. We have to endure his vulgar slanders, his fusty jests, and his hideous 'asides' on Cassio's courtesy for seventy lines (II. i. 100–76). In all of the exchanges Shakespeare is working up to the joyful moment when Othello, reunited with Desdemona, expresses in an aria of love the sense that he has reached the very peak of his emotional experience. It is a heart stopping moment but it is only seventeen lines long (II. i. 180–97). We will remember this flash of ecstasy for the rest of Othello's muddied course. We do not at this point know it but, in this brief exchange, Othello speaks more than half the lines he will direct to Desdemona before he becomes irrecoverably lost in the toils of suspicions that she has cuckolded him.

We see Iago at the extreme point of insolence when he attends to the task of reinterpreting the innocent Cassio's solicitous courtesy to Desdemona in a sinister and fantastic light for the crestfallen Roderigo. The poor trash of Venice soon accepts a role in a plot to eliminate his rival on evidence he has seen neither with his own eyes, nor, in any degree of conviction, with Iago's. That, however, is not the most remarkable example of gullibility in this scene. How can Iago best convince the audience to share his vision of a corrupt world? By showing, as he does in the soliloquy following Roderigo's departure, how easily he can swallow his own lies. He believes Cassio loves Desdemona. Come to that he loves her himself. He suspects Othello of cuckolding him with Emilia and, as an afterthought, suspects Cassio with his nightcap too (II. i. 280–306). The leisure allowed to him to strike such teasing postures oppresses the audience. We have much more of Iago than we ever want or need. He has over two-thirds of the more than 200 lines of soliloquies and asides in the play. By the time Othello is first alone on stage musing in torment (III. iii. 242–3, 258–77) Iago has already delivered six of his soliloquies. Nothing bewilders us more about the unfathomable nature of evil than Iago's playful attempts, in his dance of the seven motives, to explain himself to himself.

While Cassio performs the role of stage-drunk in Iago's undeclared play, the ensign, a wizard at doubling, undertakes a bewildering variety of roles: convivial fellow-officer encouraging Cassio to celebrate his general's marriage (II. iii. 12–43, 60–113); enthusiastic author and director explaining to us how industrious he has been in setting the lieutenant up for catastrophe (44–59); concerned spectator revealing Cassio's lamentable weakness to Montano (114–39); stage manager directing Roderigo in Cassio's tracks. His plot reaches a swift climax (140–58) and, once he has ensured that the bell arouses Othello, he is the only trusty unbiased reporter available. The review he gives of the theatrical triumph he has improvised modestly conceals the array of talents he has displayed in it.

The only exchange Othello has with Cassio, the subject of Iago's report, is a mere four lines long. Othello will not interact directly with Cassio again on stage until the very end of the play. The two characters between whom Iago forges a monstrous antagonism are involved in direct speech on stage for a mere forty lines. He is able to keep his victims apart and work on them separately in isolation. He does not even have to hunt them down. In asking for the ensign's advice, as Cassio does, they make themselves available for roles in the improvised plots he is forever hatching. Following upon his success as a drunk Cassio accepts the role, though he knows it not, of adulterous cuckolder of his general. Because Iago's contempt for us is equal to his contempt for those on stage he can cockily begin to sell to us the plausibility of his new work-in-progress:

> And what's he then that says I play the villain,
> When this advice is free I give and honest,
> Probal to thinking, and indeed the course
> To win the Moor again?

(II. iii. 319–22)

Iago demands that we acknowledge his acting skills as trusted counsellor. Shakespeare had already presented a stage-villain hissing diabolism in the role of Lucianus in *The Murder of Gonzago* with his 'Thoughts black, hands apt, drugs fit, and time agreeing' (*Hamlet*, III. ii. 245). Iago pours a different kind of poison in everyone's ears but no one on stage can ever share the kind of irritation Hamlet feels at the self-indulgent showiness of an actor mugging villainy: 'Begin murderer. Leave thy damnable faces and begin' (III. ii. 242–3). That irritation is the privilege of the audience of *Othello*. The *performance* of villainy is reserved for us in private shows, as here when Iago gives us, in what amounts to an insolent flourish of his cape, a touch of fire and brimstone villainy (II. iii. 333–6).

In Cinthio's narrative the initial events which lead to the Moor's jealousy are not organized by the ensign. The corporal falls from grace without any help. Nor does the ensign have any part in advising the corporal as to how he might repair his fortunes. The corporal does not even have to ask Disdemona to plead for him since she does it of her own accord. Shakespeare has Iago set on Cassio to sue to Desdemona, urge Emilia to persuade Desdemona to undertake the suit and promise to draw Othello out of the way while they work out their strategy. Desdemona with an admirable and predictable zeal, which nevertheless distresses the audience, explains how sincerely she will perform her role as suppliant (III. iii. 21–6).

Shakespeare invents many details as additions to Cinthio's story to justify the separation and breakdown in the relationship of the Moor and his wife. He amplifies the political context by inventing a crisis in the Venetian state which involves a battle with the Turks. He occupies Othello with the business of ensuring that peace is kept in Cyprus. Cinthio's entirely domestic story is set in a more public arena and in a severely telescoped time-frame. Shakespeare radically alters the weighting of interactions to overcome what he may have perceived to be implausible developments in the original story. Much of the success of Iago's plot depends on the scant knowledge Othello has acquired of Desdemona. His initial romantic courting has not had any time to yield place to the daily give and take of marriage. Shakespeare indicates an absence of experienced knowledge between the two in a variety of ways – the wooing, the elopement, the crisis which interrupts their wedding night and sends them in separate ships to Cyprus, and the further interruption because of Cassio's rowdiness. But he achieves his aim mainly by allowing them so little time on stage together. When Iago finally turns on Othello alone to begin the first long assault in his campaign (III. iii. 93) we have to that point seen Desdemona and her husband on stage together on five occasions, but they have shared, almost equally, less than ninety lines of direct interaction in a play which has already run over 1500 lines. At no point have we seen them alone on stage. We will, in fact, only ever see them alone together on two occasions and the second one is the murder scene. In the second half of the play Shakespeare brings husband and wife together on five occasions for some 270 lines of direct interaction, three-quarters of the stage-life they spend together which serves at every point to confirm the suspicions Iago has aroused in the Moor.

An effective contrast to the brief glimpses we have in the first half of the play of Othello and Desdemona together are the extensive interactions Iago shares with several characters as he prepares to destroy their relationship. We see him talking to Roderigo on four occasions in interactions which take up three times as many lines as those given to the moments between the Moor and his wife. The sequence devoted to the cheering up of the dismissed Cassio by Iago takes up seventy lines, and Iago, in jesting with Desdemona at the landing in Cyprus, shares almost as many lines with her as she has with Othello in their various exchanges up to the mid-point of the play. When Iago tells his general that he does not know his wife well our experience in the play dovetails at all points to make the suggestion plausible.

In Cinthio the Moor is familiar with the ways of Venice and he resides there long enough to establish domestic felicity in his marriage. Othello, by contrast, asserts that he has no experience of the social mores of domestic and civilian life (I. iii. 81–7). Shakespeare inventively enlarges on Othello's exotic nature in many of his speeches and in Iago's private analyses of the 'honest fool' he is misleading. Shakespeare had long trained his audiences to take for granted the theatrical nature of the world with its multiple levels of illusion. He develops Othello as a character to whom this European idea is alien and repellent, a quality for which there is no hint in Cinthio. Iago introduces Othello to the idea that acting is a basic practice of Venetian society manners:

> I would not have your free and noble nature,
> Out of self-bounty, be abused. Look to't.
> I know our country disposition well:
> In Venice they do let God see the pranks
> They dare not show their husbands; their best conscience
> Is not to leave't undone, but keep't unknown.
>
> (III. iii. 199–204)

Of all Iago's strategies of separation this is the most crucial, for it moves Othello into an area of which he has neither knowledge nor experience where the certain truth he seeks is, by definition, elusive. We are inclined not to impute simple gullibility to Othello as the cause of his fall because of the way everyone trusts Iago's honesty. But there are more particular reasons why Othello, who is induced to distrust Venetians, can nevertheless trust Iago. The ensign is, in the manner that Othello thinks of himself, a rough, blunt-spoken soldier who has lived on battlefields where the sophisticated role playing of civilian society has little opportunity to flourish. Iago is a man without polish more to be relished in the soldier than in the scholar. Soldiers in every age need little persuasion to look on civilians with their mannered courtesy and complex codes of behaviour as soft, effete and unreliable. Iago has shared the dangers of war with Othello when he has 'seen the cannon/When it hath blown his ranks into the air/And, like the devil, from his very arm/Puffed his own brother' (III. iv. 134–7). Othello is admirable in that he seems to have found in Desdemona a gentleness that he has placed no value on hitherto. But he is aware that there is some risk in abandoning his simple bachelor habits (I. ii. 24–8). When Iago asserts that Othello has stumbled into a theatre of illusions whose conventions he does not understand, Shakespeare has ensured, in every detail, that Othello has no accumulation of experience that would allow him to dispute it. The whole world becomes changed from what it once was and Iago offers to act as critic and commentator to help Othello spy out some flaws in the disguises adopted by those around him. Othello relies on the figure he has known and trusted longest for he 'knows all qualities, with a learned spirit/Of human dealings' (III. iii. 259–60).

In Shakespeare we feel Iago to be older and more experienced than Cassio. Cinthio makes no such distinction nor does he give any evidence that the ensign has known the Moor longer and shared many battle experiences with him. Shakespeare's Moor has developed a friendship with the young Cassio who came a-wooing with him. He is mentor and patron to one who, according to Iago, has 'never set a squadron in a field' and who has made his mark in training as a theoretician. Cinthio's ensign is superior in rank to the corporal so there is no bitter resentment about any promotion. We may surmise, without uncritically accepting Iago's views, that he was passed over by Othello because he was so much taken for granted: 'And I (of whom his eyes had seen the proof/At Rhodes, at Cyprus, and on other grounds/Christian and heathen) must be belee'd and calmed' (I. i. 28–30). The more he relies on the friend he has so long taken for granted the more he is separated from any comfortable acceptance of the newer friends who come from the treacherous Venetian world of which he has such limited experience.

The advantage Iago gains in persuading Othello that he is in a world of tricky, skilful actors is that it gives him an unchallengeable excuse for the shortage of unambiguous evidence of Desdemona's infidelity: 'Where's satisfaction?/It is impossible you should see this,/Were they as prime as goats, as hot as monkeys' (III. iii. 401–3). When Othello presses hard for 'ocular proof' Iago can only offer the next best thing – a report of a dream, a mere imitation of an action, Cassio miming and rehearsing his act of love in his sleep. This is as close as you can get to evidence in catching out the clever Venetian actors in their sins. Well, that is not quite true. There is the handkerchief. Commentators frequently point out how flimsy Iago's plot is but fail to note that were it not so flimsy it could not succeed. If at any point Iago offers Othello a fact which breaches the completely theatrical, illusionary façade he has created then he gives him a means of tearing it down. Iago cannot take Othello behind the scenes because there is no behind the scenes. Othello is separated from a world that does not exist. A piece of linen is not much but we see very clearly that, with only slightly altered circumstances, it would be enough to destroy Iago's plot.

Shakespeare invents an exotic history of associations for which Othello values the handkerchief, makes Iago's use of it daring to the point of folly, and complicates the dangers associated with the talisman far beyond anything Cinthio imagines. In the novella the ensign's wife has no contact with it, rather it is the ensign himself who, without anyone's knowledge, steals the handkerchief from Disdemona as she is distracted in the enjoyment of playing with his child. There is never, in Cinthio, any chance that this link in the plot could fail. The handkerchief completes its journey from the ensign's hand to the corporal's lodging where the Moor is brought to observe a sempstress in the window copying its design. Shakespeare organizes Iago's use of the handkerchief as a lucky, stumbling run across a minefield. The audience knows, as he does not when he receives it from Emilia, that the handkerchief Iago claims he has seen Cassio wiping his beard with earlier in the day was only minutes past in Othello's hand or pressed to his forehead by Desdemona. Though Othello has failed to register its very distinctive embroidery the audience momentarily retains hope that the napkin can be rescued from its deadly significance. When Desdemona comes on hunting for it (III. iv) we know that she was unaware of using it to soothe Othello's horn-mad brow. As Emilia fails to reveal knowledge of its whereabouts we know that this trifle light as air will become confirmation strong as proofs of holy writ. It takes only 150 lines to make the flimsiest link in Iago's plot its lynch-pin.

In embroiling Emilia in the handkerchief's varied journey Shakespeare indicates to us her ignorance of the really vicious nature of her husband. His method of increasing the density of character involvement in the handkerchief's journey not only allows Iago to survive several transits of thin ice, it also allows many opportunities for Othello to convince himself that he is ensnared by Venetian actors. The napkin passes from Desdemona's hand to Othello's to the floor, to Emilia to Iago. After it has been dropped in Cassio's lodging we see him give it to Bianca and we and Othello see her in jealousy throw it back at him. When Othello challenges Desdemona about the loss of his handkerchief she insists, as the wife does not in Cinthio, that they talk about returning Cassio to favour, refusing to let this red herring put her from her suit. It can only seem to Othello that the Venetian actress Iago has warned him of has extraordinary nerve in treating him as a cuckolded fool to his face when he talks of the evidence which makes her pretence invalid.

Shakespeare made significant changes in the peeping-Tom incident, where Othello attends to Iago's conversation with Cassio IV. i. 100–66),

as it appears in Cinthio. Cinthio's Moor does not overhear and miscon-
strue an actual conversation. He watches from a distance as the ensign
talks to the corporal and interprets guilt simply from the corporal's
gestures. Only afterwards does he hear from the ensign, who has
complete freedom to invent, the actual contents of the conversation. In
Shakespeare this painfully vivid scene demonstrates Iago's extraordinary
luck in the risky improvisations he attempts. In addition to the good
performance Iago gets from Cassio he receives the unexpected bonus of
Bianca, as a self-recruiting member of his repertory company, bringing
on the will-o'-the-wisp handkerchief as a final touch, and an addition to
Cinthio, that stones Othello's heart. The Moor sees that a slut is his wife's
chief competitor for Cassio's affections. It is the placing of this scene
which gives it such potency. In Cinthio the sequence comes much earlier
in the story just after the ensign has spread his lies and before the Moor
has been told about the handkerchief or challenged his wife about its loss.
When the Moor there, with no other 'evidence', accepts the ensign's
report of a conversation conducted out of his hearing, he is certainly
buying a pig in a poke. Shakespeare's peeping-Tom scene seems to
Othello the cast-iron, solid evidence he has been looking for, a behind-
the-scene's glimpse of the Venetian without his mask condemning
himself out of his own mouth. Othello has already heard about lecherous
dreams, about his handkerchief, and reports by Iago of Cassio's private
admissions of adultery. He has listened to his wife's denial of the loss of
the handkerchief and to her pleading for Cassio; he has been driven to the
point of seizure by his inability to catch out these Venetians. So by the
time Othello hears Cassio laughing contemptuously about the 'bauble'
who so dotes on him, the precious handkerchief the Moor accidentally
cast aside as 'too little' has grown to monstrous proportions. Tossed
around so casually by the Venetians, it becomes the very symbol of the
illusory world of feckless duplicity that Iago has created. Othello in-
teracts directly with Cassio in only three of the nine scenes in which they
share the stage together for a total of some forty lines. Here Othello
observes Iago talking for almost seventy lines with Cassio. The scene is a
vivid picture of the way Iago has separated Othello from those he trusted.

Othello makes it clear in his behaviour to Desdemona during the
welcoming of Lodovico that he is no longer taken in by Venetian
performers. He believes her response to his striking of her are the
crocodile tears of 'well-painted passion' and that she is 'obedient' only to
the task of sustaining her role (IV. i. 246–53). He wants, nevertheless to
force a direct admission of guilt from this 'cunning'st pattern of excelling
nature'. Shakespeare adds to the intolerable pressure brought to bear on

the audience by linking to our experience of Iago as such a good actor our experience of Othello as such a bad one. Only now, in the brothel scene (IV. ii), when Othello is almost completely alienated from Desdemona, does Shakespeare allow them for the first time in the play a direct interaction in which they have the stage to themselves. By contrast, up to this moment in the play Iago and Othello have shared almost 500 lines of interaction alone together. The Moor intends to catch out these Venetian actors. He will force Desdemona to be what she is by becoming an actor himself. He will pretend to be like the Cassio he thinks he has seen, a regular inhabitant of the secret, backstairs world of purchased lust. He has seen Cassio's light, frivolous behaviour with his whore but he cannot imitate it. He is so maddened by Desdemona's 'performance' as bewildered innocent that he has to abandon his role as a customer in order to assault her wildly in his own proper person as a despised husband. The cunning whore of Venice acts him off the stage. The audience has waited a long time for this scene, for it has to maintain one last hope that if Othello and Desdemona are left alone together long enough they might discover the truth. Othello spends some sixty lines alone with his wife here but we see at once that the more vehemently she denies his accusations the more he is convinced they are correct. Othello, giving money to the madame, Emilia, for his 'course', leaves the bawdy house of his imagination as he is leaving his marriage at the heavy cost of receiving none of the pleasures for which he contracted.

In his bad acting, his inability to mask his cuckold's fury, the unsubtle Othello poses an increasing threat to Iago's plot. In Cinthio the ensign's wife knows the whole nature of her husband's villainy but reveals her knowledge only long after the deaths of Disdemona and the Moor, and just after the death by torture, in connection with other plots, of the villain. Shakespeare makes the person closest to Iago ignorant of his villainy but allows her to stumble all around the truth without uncovering it in time. This allows him to develop Emilia's umabiguous loyalty and steady companionship to the gentle and increasingly isolated Desdemona. The chief harvest he reaps by altering the nature of the ensign's wife he found in Cinthio is the 'willow scene'.

It is the only scene in the play, save for the transitional II.ii and III.ii, in which Iago makes no appearance. It is the only calm scene of normal domestic behaviour. This bedroom chatter, a pause at the brink of a headlong plunge to chaos, is entirely free of any role-playing deception, or the nightmare illusions which have filled the stage for so long. In the almost 100 lines they share alone the women sustain a longer interaction than any that we see between Othello and his wife. The affection displayed between the women here prepares us for Emilia's loyalty when she returns to the bedchamber later. All of her jests about disloyalty to husbands correspond to the picture of Venetian wiles that Iago has shown to Othello. Desdemona, unlike Othello, cannot bring herself to believe that such devious behaviour is possible. Since Iago first set to work to poison Othello's mind (III. iii. 93), we have seen Othello on stage for over 800 lines, but during all the corrosive decline in the Moor's faith we have seen Desdemona with him for less than a quarter of those lines. She still has no explanation for his bewildering behaviour and resists all the suggestions of jealousy Emilia shrewdly intuits.

The more Iago is caught up in the inexorable mechanism he has set in motion the less opportunity Shakespeare gives him to strut in soliloquy, superior and separate from his victims. In the attempted murder of Cassio, he has time only for a hasty explanation to us of his problem before the juggling act of keeping everyone in separate compartments begins to break down. Iago knows that both of his wounded dupes must die, but he bungles the job. He has an urgent need to be off stage so that he can re-enter in the role of detached, innocent bystander. He takes the risk of stabbing Roderigo in front of others but leaves Cassio as a loose end in his villainy.

Othello's calmness in approaching murder is a vivid contrast to Iago's hole-and-corner ambush. We can ascribe the Moor's calm nobility (V. ii. 1–22) to the fact that he is at last master of the stage. Because Desdemona is, initially, asleep he is not enraged by another of her 'performances' of pretended innocence. For a moment he sees himself as the embodiment of justice and recaptures the essence of that magisterially calm figure who described his whole course of love to the Venetian senate. But the delay incurred in affirming his calm resolution allows Desdemona to awake and he is soon forced back, as her words indicate (V. ii. 37–8; 43–4), into his posture of enraged cuckold. This is the final turn of the screw in the pressure Shakespeare applies to the audience. He allows husband and wife as long an interaction as any they have had hitherto. Othello reveals the identity of the man he suspects, Cassio, and the nature of his evidence, the handkerchief, but he grows more and more convinced of Desdemona's guilt the longer he spends with her. If we had once wished for them to be alone to uncover Iago's lies, we now wish for someone to interrupt them before they are acted upon. Shakespeare arranges matters so that everyone else is drawn into the streets because of Iago's bungled attempt at murder. We can hope that Emilia, on her way to report it, will arrive in time. She had knocked at the door of truth several times but she finds it only seconds too late behind the bedroom door. The final irony of

Othello's confused response to Desdemona's mask occurs in her momentary revival after Emilia's entry. Her final line in which she claims to have killed herself is her one piece of deceptive acting in the play. It must seem to him one last outrageous attempt to outface him and deny him the certainty of justice in his own actions, perhaps even one final attempt to corrupt him into joining her world of lies. If her death were reported as an inexplicable suicide then her adultery and dishonour need never be uncovered, for 'their best conscience/Is not to leave't undone, but keep't unknown'. Othello rejects the mask his dying wife offers him and admits his guilt (V. ii. 130–1). It is at least partly because Othello cannot be two-faced that the Janus-headed Iago is exposed.

Shakespeare achieves the ironies and the tension by changing completely the nature of the murder as Cinthio writes it. The ensign hiding in the closet, the Moor leading his wife thither, the ensign jumping out to bludgeon her to death with a stocking full of sand, the pulling down of the roof to make it look like an accident – all of the detail is the stuff on which sensational journalism feeds. Shakespeare casts it all aside to capitalize on a rich paradox of his scenic structure. In producing a psychological and physical separation between Othello and Desdemona Iago never lets the Moor out his sight for very long. Shakespeare, however, has Iago trust Othello to undertake the murder unaided in order to provide himself with an alibi for the villainy he confidently believes is undetectable. Iago has found roles for everyone in his plots and has provided for them all, with one crucial exception, adequate motivation for his actions and for their own. He took Emilia's filching of the handkerchief for granted and gave her no excuse for his need of it. The flaw in his theatre of illusions is a failure to act his own part completely. It is to some extent his contempt for women which allows him to engineer his plot, and it is contempt for his wife which supplies the gap in his fabrications through which the truth can rush. Emilia's loyalty to her dead mistress beyond fear of or duty to her husband does not surprise us. We have seen Emilia interacting for more lines with Desdemona than with her husband and of all Iago's interactions the one given least stage-life, less even than his talks with Desdemona, is the relationship with his wife.

At the end Othello is baffled with ignorance and we, kept for so long abreast of all the nasty manoeuvres and motives at the instant of their conception, are baffled by knowledge. We can understand why Iago will remain silent. He no longer has an audience he can tease with its helplessness to interfere as a source of his power. Many explanations have been given for the recovered stature which Othello achieves at the end. In spite of all the bizarre behaviour Iago has induced in him the dignity of his ending is impressive and that is partly because our sense of detachment is undercut. When Othello shares the knowledge we have been burdened with for so long we share the amazement of his response. When he asks 'Will you, I pray, demand that demi-devil/Why he hath thus ensnared my soul and body?' (V. ii. 301–2) there is no one in the audience, let alone on stage, who can provide a satisfactory answer. In tragedy we can bear to watch characters suffering because we gain understanding. We seem to gain an understanding in *Othello* that certain things are unknowable.

It has often been asserted that Othello is simply a credulous fool, but if Shakespeare had indeed presented him so then our only recourse would be to get busy and put money in our purses. It is Iago's intention to convince us that the world is full of fools to be practised upon. Many theatregoers and critics are so convinced. It is remarkable that such people fail to recognize their kinship with Roderigo. Roderigo, with an advantage denied to Othello, sees Iago without his mask, believes he can be part of an evil plot and yet invulnerable to it, and is even willing to pay money to be convinced of the gullibility of Othello while ignoring his own. Iago has the audience on the hip because of the masterly ingenuity with which Shakespeare varies his techniques of character interaction and separation. He keeps characters apart when we want them to be together, he brings them together when we want them kept apart. He makes us aware that we are separated from the action and yet makes our torment so real that we almost wish we could talk to the characters. The one character we would like to get away from is allowed to thrust himself upon us whenever he feels like it. The more we are put in the picture the more we understand how others are kept out of it. Othello has been forced to be an audience when he wanted to be an actor, he has been an actor when he thought of himself as an audience. He has been on stage when he thought himself behind the scenes. Our eagerness to accept his rehabilitation at the end is explicable in terms of the theatrical modes of action Shakespeare juggles with. It is a bewildering irony of his technique that Othello can get himself out of this world of theatrical illusions by deceiving those around him into thinking that he is weaponless. Iago has divided Othello from himself, from his wife and from us. When the enigma of Iago recedes we are for a moment reunited with the Othello we initially encountered. When it is his cue to strike he knows it without a prompter. In his final speech and his suicide he is able, as he was before the Senate in Venice, to express his nobility and to manifest himself rightly.

Index